Printed in China

孔子学院总部赠送

Donated by Confucius Institute Headquarters

ONCE UPON A TIME IN SHANGHAI

A Jewish Woman's Journey through the 20th Century China

Rena Krasno

CHINA
INTERCONTINENTAL
PRESS

图书在版编目（CIP）数据

上海往事：1923–1949：犹太少女的中国岁月：英文／（美）瑞娜·克拉斯诺著. —北京：五洲传播出版社，2008.11
　ISBN 978-7-5085-1344-7

I. 上…
II. 瑞…
III. 上海市—地方史—史料—英文
IV. K295.1
中国版本图书馆CIP数据核字 (2008) 第064910号

ONCE UPON A TIME IN SHANGHAI

A JEWISH WOMAN'S JOURNEY THROUGH THE 20TH CENTURY CHINA

Author: Rena Krasno
Executive Editor: Wu Yamin
Art Director: Tian Lin
Publisher: China Intercontinental Press
　　　　(6 Beixiaomachang, Lianhuachi Donglu, Haidian District, Beijing 100038, China)
Printer: Beijing BOHS Color Printing Co.,Ltd.
Format: 720×965mm　1/16
Signatures: 9.5
Words: 90,000
Edition: Nov. 2008, 1st edition, 1st print run
Print Run: 1-3,500
Price: RMB 90.00 (yuan)

To Tess Johnston, Deke Ehr and all who love Shanghai.

CONTENTS

Preface

I n the spring of 1989, I met Rena Krasno in California, USA. Rena was very excited to see me, the guy from Shanghai. She asked me many questions about the city's changes and development. Her love for China and Shanghai moved me, especially when she said, "I really want to go back to my hometown—Shanghai, which I have left for 40 years."

In 1994, I got the chance to help Rena return to Shanghai. At that time, with the support of the Shanghai government, we decided to host the first international academic conference with the theme of "Jews in Shanghai". As a member of the conference's organizing committee, I suggested inviting Rena to attend and deliver a speech at the conference.

She recorded her feelings about revisiting Shanghai at the end of this book. She said that she could not express in words how excited she was upon receiving that invitation. She was trembling as the plane descended for landing. As soon as she set foot on Shanghai soil, she felt she had returned home. Rena delivered a wonderful speech at the conference. She said, her nationality aside, Shanghai was her hometown, because she was born and raised in the city. How touching is that?

In those days, Rena had been immersed in her memories and recollections. She walked along Huaihai Road (formerly Avenue Joffre) for a long time and never got tired. She revisited Aurora University (Shanghai Second Medical University in 1994) and College Municipal Français (currently Shanghai Science Hall), where had studied. She spent a lot of time in the city's old district and tasted many local snacks, such as bannock, twisted crullers and roasted sweet potatoes. Sometimes, she just sat and watched Shanghai people going about their time, living their lives. She also visited the Tower Apt. (Xiangyang South Road Junction, Huaihai Middle Road) where she was brought up. There, she recalled her parents' love for her again in her "boudoir".

She has visited the city many times since then. I can't remember how many visits she has made to Shanghai, which she called "the city of youth". I am her loyal companion during her visits. Every time, we look around the city and discuss the changes it has undergone. She will tell the graduates in the institute many stories. I will meet her when I visit Mountain View, California. I have forgotten how many times we have sat together for a long talk, without regard for passing time.

Rena is one of the Shanghai people who can't speak the local dialect. The history of Shanghai shows that it has always been an open city. People could come and go freely —sometimes, even without passports and visas. Industrialists started their businesses in Shanghai, refugees found safe haven in Shanghai, and adventurers discovered "paradise" in Shanghai. Different languages, custom, beliefs and people from all races assemble in the city. As the intersection of cultural integration, the city has become an international metropolis. Shanghai culture has developed under such circumstances. It integrates different cultures of China and other countries, and is characterized by openness and internationalism.

Rena was born in a Jewish family and brought up in Shanghai culture. It can be said that she has an integrated Chinese and Jewish cultural background. She had stayed in Israel for some time, and then worked in the United Nations for many years. She can speak six languages and has travelled many places around the world. At last, she decided to settle down in the USA.

Rena's experience reflects the competition and complementation of multiculturalism, which is developed by adopting a multitude of approaches to life rather than a single one. It's like a long river with many tributaries. Each tributary is distinctive, but they will join together at the mouth to the sea. Such experiences make Rena's works rich and varied. They have the characteristics of different cultures, with the essence of Shanghai culture welling up from deep inside.

Although the stories of Rena took place in old Shanghai, she still feels very excited about the change and development of modern Shanghai.

Thirty years ago, China started to carry out the reform and opening policies. It opened up to the world and began to boom. Under such circumstances, the openness and internationalism of Shanghai culture was highlighted and brought to new heights. That is why there are so many people from other parts of China and other countries in Shanghai today. Figures from 2002 indicate that 2.1 million foreigners came to Shanghai and stayed here for a certain period that year. It is predicted that 70 million people will visit the city by 2010, when the Shanghai World Expo is slated to run. It is said that Shanghai now has more than 150,000 foreigners, nearly equal to the peak number in the 1930s.

These people from other areas of China and other countries have become the "new Shanghai people". The cultures they bring to Shanghai make Shanghai culture more attractive and have become the new landmarks of the city's development.

Meanwhile, many Chinese people, especially those from Shanghai, have gone abroad for business, education or travel. This drives Shanghai's cultural development, making the city more influential in the world.

All of these factors provide new elements for Rena's books and encourage her to write more excellent works.

As a good friend of Rena, I am so proud of her for having written so many excellent works. She is now over 80 years old. But she told me she had another four books to be published later. I know they must contain many stories about Shanghai.

I truly hope Rena will be able to keep her youth forever and write more stories about Shanghai.

Pan Guang

Prof. & Dean, Center of Jewish Studies Shanghai (CJSS) at SASS
November 6, 2008

From you have I been absent in the spring,

When proud-pied April, dressed in all his trim,

Hath put a spirit of youth in everything,

That heavy Saturn laughed and leaped with him.

William Shakespeare

Chapter 1

BEGINNINGS

I was born in Shanghai in December 1923 and left the city of my birth in 1949.

When I was young, Great Britain was the greatest foreign power in China. It had initiated the Opium War and defeated the Chinese who possessed neither modern warships nor armor. Until then, trade between England and China was one-sided. Great Britain imported silk, spices, objects of art in great quantities, but China was not interested in buying anything from Europe. The result: British ships sailed to China loaded with bricks for ballast, and returned packed with Chinese merchandise. These red bricks were eventually used to build the British Consulate in Shanghai.

The *Treaty of Nanking* in 1842 awarded the victor the status of "Most Favored Nation." Five Treaty ports were created: Shanghai, Foochow (Fuzhou), Amoy (Xiamen), Canton (Guangzhou), and Ningpo (Ningbo). As time went by, the number of Treaty ports in China reached 80. The U.S. and France followed shortly after with bullying tactics and forced the Chinese to give them advantages similar to those of the British. In the concessions, each country established its own courts of justice, its own schools, its own police force, army, hospitals and clubs. Thus, Shanghai was divided into three: the International Settlement (British and American), the French Concession and the Chinese City.

Shanghai became open to all foreign imports, including high grade Bengal opium. Profits were immense.

My parents were Stateless Russian Jews. My mother had arrived from

Author with her mother and little sister, 1926. This is the photo for their identity card.

Siberia as a small child of 8 in 1912 with her parents and five siblings, to escape from cruel pogroms. Shortly after their arrival in the midst of a cholera epidemic, my grandfather came across a desperately ill Chinese man on the street, put him in a rickshaw and took him to the nearest hospital. The old man survived his cholera attack, but my grandfather—still a young man in his 40's—contracted the disease and died several days later. My grandmother, Ekaterina Abramovna, who knew no English and had no skills, started cooking cheap meals for poverty stricken Russian Jewish refugees. That is how my father eventually met my mother when having lunch at my future grandmother's home. They got married in 1921.

Ekaterina Abramovna who had got married when she was only 15 years old and her husband 15½, had had no education. Her ambition was for her sons to graduate universities in the United States. Her daughters had to start working early. When my mother Aida was small she was sent to a Catholic boarding school near the Bund. When I was little, she loved to tell me a true story about a "dragon."

One day, when my mother was about 9 years old, her classmates and she heard a big racket outside on the street: shouting, clanging of metal on metal, policeman's whistles and the loud ringing of a fire engine. In spite of the teacher's efforts to keep them quiet, they all rushed to the windows. A green alligator was ambling along the street followed by groups of noisy Chinese banging on saucepans of all sizes. Some pointed to it shouting "Dragon! Dragon!" A frightened policeman was frantically trying to regulate the traffic and a red fire engine was attempting to weave through the crowd.

It appeared that the alligator had crawled unseen into one of the opium crates as it was being packed for shipment to Shanghai. Then, when the case was broken open upon arrival, the alligator scrambled out and calmly went on its way. I was later told that "the dragon" was eventually stuffed and displayed in one of Shanghai's museums.

My mother started working as a typist when she was 13. She was very energetic, optimistic, hard-working and kind-hearted.

My father arrived in Shanghai at the age of 21 from Vladivostok, Siberia, on his way to Palestine. He was a Zionist strongly believing that Jews who were persecuted throughout the world had to have their own country. Unfortunately, he suffered an appendicitis attack in Shanghai, had to be operated and could not continue his trip. Like many other Russian Jewish refugees, he was penniless.

As far back as I could remember, I adored my father, David Rabinovich. He was a poet, a writer, a life-long idealist. When he got stuck in Shanghai, he learned English as quickly as possible. To survive, he gave Russian lessons to group Chinese students for a small fee. One day, one of his students, asked my father if he would be interested to meet Dr. Sun Yat-sen (1866–1925) whom my father greatly admired. If so, her prominent uncle could set up an appointment for him. Of course, my father was delighted. When Dr. Sun approached him in the living room of his home where many Chinese were waiting to speak to him, my father stammered nervously his sympathy and respect for the national movement in China, and mentioned that he was a Jew. Dr. Sun responded that he had long admired the perseverance and courage of the Jewish people during centuries of persecution.

When my father had become a respected Jewish leader in Shanghai, he met General Ma, Sun Yat-sen's famous bodyguard. General Ma was born Morris

Editorial staff of *Our Life*, 1941. Author's father, David B.Rabinovich on the left.

Cohen. Later he earned the nickname 2-Gun Cohen because of the two pistols he always carried quite visibly. Cohen was the son of a poor London synagogue warden. His parents could not control him as a rebellious youth and sent him to Canada to a farm, which he quickly left. Soon he met Chinese revolutionaries who introduced him to Dr. Sun Yat-sen to whom Cohen became very attached and whom he served with the utmost loyalty. When Sun Yat-sen came to power he made 2-Gun a General, General Ma. During World-War II, Cohen went to Hong Kong to rescue Sun Yat-sen's wife who had established the China Defence League there. The Japanese arrested him and sent him to a concentration camp, which he managed to survive. 2-Gun often said:

"I only cried twice in my life. Once when my father died and when Dr. Sun Yat-sen died!"

The British had separate Girls' Schools and Boys' Schools. Public School girls wore white blouses and dark blue tunics. Purple was the elegant color of the Cathedral School. Sports were encouraged. To graduate High School, students had to pass the Cambridge Matriculation Examination.

British companies wrote "marriage" rules into contracts with bachelor employees. They had to agree to serve the company 3, 5 or even 7 years before getting married. Then their boss would usually interview the young lady and decide if she would make a suitable wife. If the woman was Chinese, or mixed blood, usually no marriage permission was given. In some cases, the young man would be sent back to England, or transferred to a distant outpost to separate him from his beloved.

British citizens organized parades and celebrations on the King's birthday—first, Queen Elizabeth's grandfather, then her father ruled England. Races using swift Mongolian ponies were very popular, as were paper hunts, cricket and soccer. To satisfy cultural needs, the British founded the S.A.D.S.—the Shanghai Amateur Dramatic Society—whose performances were of a remarkably high standard. Opening nights at the attractive Lyceum Theatre (which still exists today) were important social events. Theatregoers turned up formally dressed and the ambience was one of excited anticipation. Seldom was the audience disappointed.

The British referred to Shanghai as the "Muddy Flats." The Whangpoo (Huangpu) River embankment had not been reinforced as yet. Later, the river bank was consolidated in a process called "bunding." This is where the name of the large avenue along the river, the famous Bund, originates. Later, when magnificent high-rise buildings were planned along the Bund, a British company, Dodwell & Co., where my father was employed, imported enormous tree trunks from the U.S. to reinforce their foundations.

In the late 1850's, the U.S. leased land north of the British areas. The United States never took over formally this land but later combined it with British owned land to form the International Settlement.

Like the British, the Americans in Shanghai had their own court of justice, their own church, their own school and their own clubs. The U.S. 4th Marines, many of whom later lost their lives when the Pacific War started, were stationed in Shanghai.

The Americans opened the first foreign school for Chinese girls in Shanghai in 1892, the McTyeire School. Its aim: to teach the best of both Eastern and Western culture. Its headmistress, Laura Askew Haywood, promised parents that their daughters would be safe in her school since "no man would be allowed beyond its gate."

Later, the Shanghai American School was established. During the Japanese occupation of Shanghai, the American School building on Avenue Petain (Beidang Lu today) became the headquarters of the feared Japanese Kempetai (military police).

In 1848, when Monsieur de Montigny, the first French Consul, arrived in Shanghai, the entire population of the French colony was only 87.

The largest French company was Olivier-Chine, which had huge godowns (warehouses) and workshops employing 300 Chinese. The job of the Chinese was, amazingly, to crack eggs using the yolks to soften leather sold locally and the whites to export for nougat manufacture in Southwest France. It is said the average coolie broke 2,200 eggs a day and the expert men as many as 4,200!

Felix Bouvier was called the "Uncrowned French King of Shanghai." He built the Canidrome (today the site of a flower market) where dog races were held. The inauguration of the Canidrome took place in 1928. A frenzied crowd of 50,000 attended. In addition to the Canidrome, Bouvier constructed the Hai Alai (Jai Alai in Spanish, a Basque gambling sport) auditorium. Gamblers made or lost huge fortunes in both enterprises.

Like the British and the Americans, the French had their own courts of justice, their own troops (mainly Indochinese), their own police (which included White Russians) and their own tax system. The biggest holiday in the French Concession took place on July 14th, Bastille Day, which had marked the start of the French Revolution. French flags fluttered in the streets, the French army band marched down Avenue Joffre (Huaihai Lu today), the Concession's main street, loudly playing the Marseillaise. Schools, offices and banks were closed. Celebrations took place in the art-deco-style French Club (today part of the Garden Hotel).

Sometimes problems arose between the Great Powers in Shanghai; one such was the question of the ricksha. It appears that the ricksha originated in Japan when a U.S. missionary in Yokohama—a certain Rev. Globe—had a baby carriage converted for his invalid wife in 1869 and thus produced a prototype of the ricksha, called by the Japanese *jinrikisha*. The word derives from the Japanese: *jin* meaning power, *riki* meaning man, and *sha* meaning vehicle. Not to be outdone, the French declared that it was a Frenchman named Menard who introduced the ricksha when he came to Shanghai in 1873 from Japan.

A rickshaw coolie waiting for customer, 1940.

Menard had submitted to the French Municipal Council "a project for the establishment of a service of small hand carts for passenger traffic in the Concessions," demanding a 10-year monopoly for himself. Sensing the prospect of high profits, the French Municipal Council welcomed the introduction of rickshas, but would not accede to Menard's wish for sole rights. They said that agreement had first to be sought from the British in accordance with Treaty regulations between the colonial powers. After lengthy negotiations and postponements, the French Council obtained a satisfactory contract from which they derived a fat profit, the British received a share, Menard was pacified with an outright payment, and… a new class of exploited Chinese was created.

My family lived in the French Concession (popularly dubbed "Frenchtown"), so I attended the College Municipal Français (French Municipal College). The language of instruction was French. English was the second language. Throughout my education, at the College and later at the University, I did not attend a single class on Chinese language, history, geography, art or culture. For all intents and purposes, I was living and studying in Paris! Our important examination papers were sent to the Sorbonne for evaluation and our diplomas were fully recognized in France. Although I later learned a number of languages and became a simultaneous interpreter for the UNESCO, to my great sorrow, I did not speak Chinese. Neither did the majority of my friends.

Chapter 2

EARLY CHILDHOOD

My earliest memories go back to when I was two years old.

My father and his twin brother Gabriel who had arrived in Shanghai in 1921 later sent for their parents who had remained behind in Vladivostok. Their father, Boris Rabinovich, was a very religious man. Many people honored him calling him Rabbi (a Jewish learned man qualified to teach Jewish law). My grandmother, Maria Oshervna, whom I simply called Babushka (Russian for grandmother) had to work hard in Siberia. While her husband was dedicated to studying the Bible and other sacred scriptures, she became a businesswoman in order to provide for her family. She had four sons (two of whom, unfortunately, died in their childhood).

I remember my grandfather, who appeared very tall to me, lying on his hands and knees on the floor, his long white beard brushing the carpet while I squealed and rode on his back pretending he was a pony.

In Vladivostok, my grandfather was a close friend of Rabbi Meir Ashkenazi. They worked night and day to help various Jews who had been harmed by anti-semitic pogroms. After my grandfather arrived in Shanghai, he persuaded Rabbi Ashkenazi and his wife to join him.

Russian Jews were too poor to buy a building for a synagogue, so they rented one in Hongkew (Hongkou) and my uncle redesigned its interior. It was named Ohel Moshe, in honor of one of the first Russian Jewish immigrant leaders in Shanghai, Moshe Greenberg.

Author (right of the first line) at Masquerade Party.

Rabbi Meir Ashkenazi became the synagogue's first Rabbi. Sadly, the first funeral service he performed was for my grandfather who died when I was three years old.

Over 75 years later, I learned from an article in an English language Shanghai newspaper, that the Foreign Affairs Office of Hongkou District, Shanghai, was considering the renovation of Ohel Moshe, bringing it back to its former condition. Uncle Gava (pet name in Russian for Gabriel) had passed away but I immediately phoned his widow and daughter in Israel, asking them for a copy of the original blueprint. Miraculously, they found it and I sent a copy to the Foreign Affairs Office. A very warm exchange of emails ensued. The FAO was delighted to receive the 1926 blueprint and asked me for more materials on my uncle. I forwarded to them his portrait and some other old Shanghai documents in Chinese, as well as material I thought would be of interest to them. The synagogue was renamed Ohel Moshe

Jewish Refugee Museum.

In November 2007, when I visited Shanghai for a series of lectures and for the signing of two of my books that had appeared in Chinese, I visited Ohel Moshe. It was a very emotional meeting. I was greeted by representatives of the FAO as well as by the architect, designer and other specialists involved in the reconstruction of the synagogue. On June 6, 2008, Ohel Moshe celebrated the 60ᵗʰ anniversary of Israel's Independence with an exhibit. This was a cooperative effort between the Shanghai Foreign Affairs Office and the Consulate General of Israel. For this occasion, I have collected and sent FAO an added number of films and documents.

When I was little, my greatest adventure was to go to the Jessfield Park (Zhongshan Park today—called after Dr. Sun Yat-sen's name in Mandarin). It appeared to me to be located very far away in the International Settlement, a long bus ride from the French Concession to Yuyuen Rd (Yuyuan Lu today). The most exciting part was that they had a little zoo. There were lots of rabbits, which I loved, funny monkeys, beautiful birds with brightly colored feathers, and two big bears who frightened me.

Many Chinese children played in the park. Some flew kites on the lawns— beautiful kites in shapes of dragons and eagles floating high up in the sky. The children came with their amahs. Many amahs had bound feet (I called them "small feetie amah") and they had a hard time chasing the energetic little boys and girls who ran non-stop. My cousin, who was a year older than I, was a very naughty boy and kept escaping from his "small feetie" amah, Ah Lee. His pet name was Abrania (Russian for Abraham). There was no way that Ah Lee could pronounce that. She called him "Umbalela" (umbrella) which always made us laugh.

In summer, there were weekly night concerts of the Shanghai Municipal Orchestra which, of course, I was not allowed to attend. Jessfield Park had an interesting history. It was named after a little girl whom a wealthy American had saved from her mother who beat her mercilessly. Most probably money had exchanged hands. Eventually, as the child, whom he named Jessie, grew older, he sent her to the United States to College. When she returned as a refined and educated young lady, her guardian fell in love with her, married her and named a large piece of land after her: Jessfield Park.

During the Japanese occupation of Shanghai, Japanese soldiers completely

Author at age 4, 1927.

took over Jessfield Park. Perhaps one of the reasons for their presence was a nearby important railway station.

On the other side of the park was St. John's University. Students had to cross the park to reach their classes. At the gate of the Jessfield stood a Japanese guard to whom they had to show their student pass. Since everyone traveled at the time by bicycle, they left their bikes at the entrance of the park and had to go directly to the University. No loitering.

When I was 5 years old, I was sent to the kindergarten of the College Municipal Français, which most people simply called "French School" in English. It was a beautiful building on Route Vallon (Nanchang Lu today), which was built originally as a French club. In 1926, the French School was installed there. I stared at the long, gracious beige building with protruding two ends and thought:

"This is a kind mother who is welcoming me with open arms!"

All the teachers spoke French and we learned to sing French songs.

Even at this early age we were taught that work was important. I still remember the words and the tune of a song we little kids used to sing with great enthusiasm:

"Travaillons, mamie en chantant
Travaillons, youp! C'est la vie! "

(Let's work, mamie, and sing

Let's work, yoop! That's Life!)

It was quite different from the popular poem under the picture of an adorable English girl in the Wonder Book for Children:

"Little Indian, Sioux or Crow,
Little frosty Eskimo,
Little Turk or Japanese,
Oh don't you wish that you were me?"

I did not last long in kindergarten and was first transferred for a short

Ohel Moshe Jewish Refugee Museum, built according to the blueprint of author's uncle in 1926.

while to a "Transition" class, then to the First Grade. Actually, since our school was entirely based on the French educational system and had a curriculum identical to that in France, the First Grade was called "Onzieme" (Eleventh Grade). Then the numbers of the classes went all the way down to the Deuxieme (Second Grade). The Deuxieme was the highest grade from which students graduated after taking the French written and oral Brevet Elementaire examination. The written exams were sent to France for evaluation and students had to wait for a while to get results.

I was the youngest pupil in class when I passed my Brevet Elementaire (the High School Graduating Examination). Luckily for me I was born in December and nobody below the age of 15 was allowed to take the examination, unless they turned at least 15 within the year. Had I been born a month later, I would have had to spend an additional year at school.

The College Municipal Français was a "mixed" school, attended by both boys and girls. In class, we sat together but the playground was divided into two by removable wooden barriers: girls on one side and boys on the other. The girls walked around during recreation or rode the Pas-de-Géants (Giant Steps) which were tall poles with four thick ropes hanging down from a turning platform with hooks. At the ends of the ropes hung comfortable leather covered nooses. The girls would stick one leg into the noose and then start running, skipping high, the swift movement carrying them flying upwards. The Pas-de-Géants were very popular: girls eagerly lined up for a chance to ride them. However, this ended one day, when a very close friend of mine somehow hit the pole from a height and died of a hemorrhage. The ropes were removed forever and the poles were a reminder of the first big tragedy in my life.

The boys, on their side of the playground mainly seemed to be occupied kicking a football and running around. It was not considered proper for girls to walk too close to the separating wooden barriers and look at the boys. The boys, on their part always appeared to be too interested in soccer to "waste" their time on girls!

We had very few Chinese, or other Asian students at school. Most of the boys and girls were either French or Stateless Russian, with a handful of other nationalities. The daughter of a former Chinese Ambassador to Paris attended some of my later classes. Her older sister was in a class above her. They had a brother who went to a prominent Chinese school according to their father's decision. Once, in one of the lower classes we also had a Vietnamese boy in our class.

However, the school was very watchful of the behavior of boys and girls. Later, in the higher classes, when we had to go up the stairs to the science laboratory, boys were told to walk up first. Why? Because if they went behind the girls they might look up their skirts!! Probably most boys had never considered this possibility but it gave them ideas!

Our prize-giving days were remarkable. Since I was a good pupil, I always awaited them with great anticipation, especially since we were given one book for each subject in which we had the first or second place. Besides, there were additional prizes, such as the Prix Audigier which was awarded in the Huitieme (Eighth Grade) to the most popular student and which to my great joy I won. I loved my prize: a thick book of French comics. Additional prizes were awarded for the best pupil in class, the second best pupil and the pupil in third place. They were given the prize of the Alliance Française. The Alliance Française (which still exists) is an association founded in 1883 to spread French influence throughout the world by propagating French education.

When I was 5 years old, my little sister Alla was born. I remember my mother and father going to the hospital and my Babushka sitting with me and trying to distract me. I did not know what really was happening but was told my mother would bring me home a sister or a brother. Babushka promised me at the time my dream party dress made of pale blue taffeta, with a wide skirt, at the hem of which were sewed tiny bells that tinkled as I walked! She also said one day, when she won the lottery, she would get me a doll that could open and close its eyes (a great novelty!) and a doll's house as well. Alas, none of these dreams ever came true, possibly because my Babushka never did win the lottery!

Chapter 3

TEA TIME

Mid-afternoon in Shanghai was tea time. Children returning from school would be served tea with milk, cookies and pastries. Their mothers either joined them or would gather with friends in the many teashops and numerous smart hotels throughout the city for an hour of chatting and relaxation. Working men had no time to join them.

Afternoon tea was a British custom promoted in Shanghai. In 1658, tea was first advertised in a London newspaper and described as a "China Drink." Tea was first imported to England from China and later from India and Ceylon (now Sri Lanka).

My father, who was employed by a British Company often mentioned with great pride:

"Dodwell's was one of the first companies to import Chinese tea to London in the 17th Century. Later, British tea clippers had races every year to be the first to land with the season's teas in the London docks. People were very excited when their tea cargo arrived from China, mainly departing from Shanghai. The tea market went up like a rocket!"

My sister and I used to laugh aloud at the story my father told us about Chinese tea being shipped to W. Wissotsky & Co. in Moscow by Dodwell & Co.

"In the earliest days of the Russian business," father said, "most of China tea traveled to Russia by camel train—a journey that took several months. The tea was packed in strong hessian-cloth sacks and loaded on camels' backs for the long trek. The camels sweated from the hard work and some of this moisture was absorbed through the cloth sacks into the tea. It added a special flavor to the tea to which the Russians became accustomed, not having any idea where it came from. When trains started running, British turned to this fast modern transportation for their cargo but were surprised when their Russian customers complained: 'Something is wrong with your tea. It does not taste as good!' To avoid the problem and recapture the old flavor, Dodwell's started adding camel hairs in their packages of tea bricks. Each brick was about 9½ inches long, 6½ inches wide, about 1 inch thick and weighed about 2½ pounds. Russians loved China tea. Everyone who could afford it drank it."

My father was served every morning a tall glass of very strong tea set in a silver holder with his breakfast. He would check its color carefully and send it back to the kitchen if it was not dark enough. My mother always had tea served in a porcelain cup with a slice of lemon. Old China Hands (foreign residents in old-time China) firmly declared that the only real tea in the world is China tea. They mocked those who added milk to their tea, calling them barbarians.

One of the favorite games of all little girls was making a tea party for their dolls. There was no plastic at the time, so my tea-set was made of painted metal: bright yellow with tiny flowers around the rims of the cups, the sugar and milk pot and the tea jar. When the weather was fine, we sat outside pretending leaves and grass were pastries, and water was tea. Some of us stuck out our little fingers when we held the cups, as we had seen pretentious ladies do. We even pretended to have adult conversations:

"Was your child good today?"

"No, my amah said he was very naughty so I punished him by making him stand in the corner."

Then we would look at each other with wise expressions and solemnly shake our heads.

Ladies loved to dress up and go for tea to their favorite spot on the Bund, the Palace Hotel (today it is the South Building of the Peace Hotel), where they were served tiny sandwiches on soft white bread, crumpets and tiny jewel-like pastry. "Foreignized" Chinese ladies also enjoyed having tea there. I thought Chinese ladies were the most beautiful women in the world:

Advertisement of Nivea Cream on Avenue Joffre, 1940.

most were slim, with wonderful straight posture and lovely legs. They wore straight gowns with high collars and short sleeves showing off slender smooth arms. The dresses, made in delicate silk or brocade, were slit from the ankle to the knee to reveal the finest silk stockings.

My father told me that an Englishman in his office smiled sarcastically when speaking of women drinking tea. Men knew what real tea was, he claimed.

"Men drink their tea straight! True connoisseurs don't even put in sugar," he affirmed. "But milk, lemon! Gods! Only a barbarian would dream of ruining China tea with such additions!"

Chapter 4

WALKING TO SCHOOL

I always left early for school. On the way I would pick up one or two friends and we would chat and laugh, walking slowly. We saved the money our parents gave us for tram fare to buy, what we called, "tucks." I believe we got this word from the British school story books we ravenously read, where children always seemed to be gobbling some kind of delicacies. Our "tucks" were Chinese.

On the way to school, stood a friendly Chinese man with a cart, on which he displayed his wares. On the side were smallish squares of Chinese newspapers which he would roll up in small cones for peanuts, dried melon seeds, pumpkin seeds, or sunflower seeds... And there was the greatest treat of all: pickled mango, a sticky, delicious brownish orange concoction that we seldom bought because it was too expensive. A cone of nuts or seeds cost 3 coppers and, alas, I really don't remember what the mango cost. The reason is that I seldom purchased it because of its high price. At the time, 300 coppers made one Chinese dollar. The mango must have cost 5 or 6 coppers. Too exorbitant for me!

On the way to school, numerous beggars on the sidewalk were unpleasant presences. To avoid them, we would step down from the pavement to the street where rickshas and bicycles were speeding. Most of the beggars were infested with lice, some had gaping wounds, and others appeared to be semi-conscious, on the verge of death. On the larger streets, like Nanking Road (Nanjing Lu today), disabled beggars would hobble after foreigners with outstretched dirty hands asking for money and weeping beggar women

Little beggar, painted by Austrian artist Friedrich Schiff.

would sit with screaming babies (it was said some secretly poked the children with needles to make they cry louder). Indeed, a distressing scene!

Occasionally, in the early hours of the day, the police would round up beggars and ship them across to the other side of the Whangpoo River. There, at the time, one could see only fields and a limited number of warehouses (today it is a modern metropolis!). However, after a short absence, the beggars would always return.

Apparently, there is no concrete proof but it does seem to be true that a very well-organized Beggars' Guild existed in Shanghai. It was said that its ruler was a powerful mystery man, a beggar "King" said to rule his "people" with a firm, strong, just hand. In good time before a big wedding, feast, or other celebration was to take place, a representative of the beggars would arrive with a warning: unless he were paid a good amount of money, the scariest cripples, would huddle at the entrance of the event wailing loudly. Many shop owners also had to pay regular fees to keep beggars away from their entrance. There was some talk about attempts of the foreign settlements to prevent this sad state of affairs by offering beggar guild leaders financial and medical assistance. However, the beggar "King" firmly rejected the foreigners' "insufficient" terms as unsatisfactory.

A friend of mine told me an amusing story. Once during the early Japanese occupation, her father sent her older sister with a coupon and money to pick up a loaf of bread at a nearby bakery. Her sister selected the loaf carefully since it had to be divided among the members of their large family. When she stepped out of the bakery, a beggar passed close to her, snatched the loaf from under her arm and disappeared. The poor girl burst out crying and returned home with tears streaming down her face. Her father tried to console her, but she kept feeling guilty about having deprived her parents and siblings of their daily bread.

One day, without telling anyone, she decided to take revenge on the beggar. She took some garbage and wrapped it in paper in the shape of a loaf of bread. She knew that the beggar thief was always loitering somewhere in their area. She then hid the parcel in her coat, went to the bakery for a few minutes and stepped out with the package openly displayed in the crook of her arm. She had guessed right! The beggar appeared from nowhere, snatched the "loaf" and took off with it. The girl returned home laughing,

Beggars.

finally rid of her guilt!

We did ride trams to school when the weather was bad: rain, sleet, and strong winds. The French Tramways Company was created in 1906 and was named 'La Compagnie Française de Tramways et Eclairage' (English translation: the French Company of Tramways and Lighting). Various problems arose for the next 22 years and the company almost closed down. Finally, in 1928, with improved leadership, it became one of the most flourishing French enterprises in Shanghai. By 1936, its number of employees increased to some twenty Russians and an equal number of Portuguese, some fifty Frenchmen and 1,500–2,000 Chinese. A good source for what was considered at the time decent employment. The tram rails cut right through Avenue Joffre.

A funny story is told about two Polish Jewish refugee newcomers who rode a tram in 1939 and were discussing in Yiddish how to reach the Ohel Rachel Synagogue. They were amazed to hear the Chinese ticket seller who stood near them suddenly give them instructions in fluent Yiddish, a Judeo-German language spoken by Jews in European towns and villages. It appears the railway employee had worked for a number of years as a houseboy for an old Jewish woman who spoke only Yiddish. Loyally, he remained with her until her death and Yiddish was the only foreign language he knew! The Polish refugees stared at him in amazement and then one said to the other:

"The Chinese people are really brilliant! Nothing is too hard for them!"

At the beginning of the Japanese occupation, my family lived on the top floor of a six-storey building, the Tower Apts., on Avenue Joffre. This building has been torn down several years ago. Some 10 yards in front of our apartment was a tram stop. One day, I was looking out of our window, waiting for my father's return by tram from a meeting. To my fear, I noticed a Japanese soldier standing at the station. When the tram stopped, he beckoned roughly to all the passengers to get out. The vehicle emptied and the people, foreign and Chinese lined up. My father was among them. The soldier started walking by the line, stopping from time to time and slapping, apparently at random, several men hard on the face. My heart squeezed wildly and I told myself:

"If he dares slap papa, if he dares, I will rush down the elevator, run out and hit him!"

Knowing my passionate character, I would have done so. Luckily, he did not touch my father. I would most definitely not have survived this insult to a representative of Emperor Hirohito!

Chapter 5

PIDGIN ENGLISH

Pidgin English did not, as many believe, start in Shanghai. It originated in Canton where foreign trade developed in the 18th Century. Pidgin later traveled to Shanghai and all the way up the China coast. Most foreigners did not attempt to learn Chinese, an effort they considered too difficult and unnecessary. In fact, many arrogant colonials believed that Asians and others had to learn their language. Actually Pidgin was not based on mispronounced English alone but contained words from various countries whose traders did business with China: Portuguese, Indian and so on. The word "Pidgin" is a corruption of the word "business," which many Chinese pronounced somewhat like "peejeness."

At first, travelers arriving in Shanghai thought all one had to do to speak Pidgin was simply to add the sound of "ee" to English words. They were wrong. It was more complicated. For example, *talkee he* meant "tell him," *bye-m-bye makee pay* meant "I'll pay later," *catchee chop chop* meant "get it quickly," *topside* stood for "upstairs," *bottomside* for "downstairs," and *savee* (from Portuguese *saber*) *box* for "brain."

A friend of mine called a couple and the houseboy answered the phone:

Friend: "Master home?"

Boy: "Masta no home."

Friend: "Missy home?"

Boy: "Missee no home."

Friend: "They go out together?"

Boy: "No! They walkee three-gether. They catchee one piece mo' man."

(Three of them went together. They had another person with them).

Comprador in Shanghai, painted by Austrian artist Friedrich Schiff.

Our cook, when he went to the market, would ask my mother:

"Missee wanchee (want) me buy walkee-walkee (live) fishee?"

Or, for instance take the word *maskee*, which derived from the Portuguese "mas que," more than. It implied things could be worse and eventually took on the meaning "never mind" in Shanghai. This became a word commonly used by all kinds of foreigners. *Maskee* embodied Shanghai's spirit: all difficulties would be overcome, one should not worry. Both Chinese and foreigners would use it routinely: from coolies to bank presidents, from children to professionals of all classes. It was an optimistic expression suggesting things could have been worse.

One day, I heard an amah tell a small child who had broken a porcelain cup:

"Maskee. Me no talkee Missee." (Never mind! I won't tell your mother). "Kitchen sidee plentee mo' cupee." (There are many more cups in the kitchen).

Some Indian words became an integral part of Pidgin. Such, for example, were *tiffin* (lunch) and *godown* (warehouse). Others derived from Chinese, such as *chow* (food) and *chop* (stamp), and yet others from Portuguese such as *savy* (know). Pidgin, discarded all grammar, and used "my" for me, "goodie, more goodie, more more goodie" for good, better and best.

When I was a teen-ager, I read a funny story in the *Readers' Digest*. Wellington Koo (1888–1985), the famous Chinese diplomat, was abroad at a large international dinner. After soup was served, his foreign neighbor asked him politely:

"Likee soupee?"

Wellington Koo smiled and nodded politely. A short time later, he stood up and made a brilliant speech in perfect English. It was greeted with enthusiastic applause. As he sat down, he asked his neighbor:

"Likee speechee?"

Even my father's very wealthy comprador spoke Pidgin. The word *comprador* comes from the Portuguese *comprar*, to buy. The Portuguese had been among the earliest foreign traders in China and left their mark in many ways. Compradors served as a middleman between non-Chinese speaking foreigners and the Chinese market. They played a preponderant role, made a great deal of money on commissions and were very loyal to the firms that employed them. No contract was ever signed between a comprador and a foreign company. Everything was built on absolute trust. Thus, it was a strong relationship that worked to the advantage of both parties. The comprador symbolized old-fashioned Chinese honor, a century's old tradition.

All the comprador had to say regarding a projected investment was either "Can do!" or "No can do!" There was no "squeeze" (overcharging) in Pidgin. It is said that a comprador knew no more than a couple hundred words in Pidgin, English or Portuguese, but this sufficed to carry out the most complicated negotiations.

My father respected his Dodwell comprador very much. He praised his business sense, his loyalty, his determination and his supervision of the honesty of Chinese staff in the department with which he dealt. However, there was no social exchange whatsoever between them. This was true of all cases between compradors and foreigners for whom they served as go-betweens. In short, the relationship was one of pure business. The comprador system lasted until the end of World War II and then slowly dissipated.

Once I went with my father to Van Shing Grocery on Avenue Joffre whom Dodwell's supplied with canned Libby's goods, Sperry flour and other food items. His comprador happened to be there. Both greeted each other with sincere joy and affection. Later, I asked my father who was the Chinese gentleman who had acted so friendly. My father replied:

"That was my comprador. One of the most honest and dependable men

Nanking Road in the 1930s.

I ever met. He only speaks Pidgin English, but that does not matter. Our relationship is one of complete trust and respect."

Chapter 6

TAILORS

Very few foreign women bought ready-made clothes in Shanghai. Some, the wealthier, "High Society" ladies purchased suits and dresses at expensive boutiques in the Cathay Hotel Arcade, or at the "Graymauve Salon" in the French Concession. Generally, women had their own Chinese tailors who came to the house, recommended either by friends, by a houseboy or amah. The Chinese tailors made clothes that really fit and looked smart.

When I was a teen-ager the tailor who came to our house was named Wu. He was a thin, nervous man, smelt of garlic and arrived equipped with a box of pins, a measuring tape, a ragged notebook and a pencil. He never used a pattern. Where had he learned his skills? That was a mystery. None of the women I knew could even imagine how their tailors were able to make elegant clothing for foreign customers. They spoke only limited Pidgin English, but did have a sense of confidence and pride in their profession. It reminded me of Chinese cooks, who prepared exquisite French, English, Italian, German, Russian meals without ever eating them. Their own meals consisted exclusively of simple Chinese dishes. Yet, they knew how to cater to the tastes of various foreigners.

Personally, I never owned fashion magazines. At the time, my favorite actress was Deanna Durbin. She had a glorious voice, a charming smile, shiny eyes and … we shared the same birthday, December 4, although she was 2 years my senior. I loved everything about her and all her clothes. When

Shanghai tailor speaking Pidgin English, painted by Austrian artist Friedrich Schiff.

I saw a photo of her in an outfit I admired, I would cut it out from the Sunday paper, or an old movie magazine and keep it. Every year my mother ordered a new outfit for me for Prize Giving Day and, invariably, I chose something Deanna wore. My favorite was a navy blue skirt, bolero and white blouse I wore when I graduated High School. My mother bought me the necessary length of heavy navy blue cotton for the skirt and bolero to which I added a white hat, with dark blue ribbon bought in a Chinese store on Avenue Joffre. My! Did I feel elegant! Wu would look at the picture of the outfit I wanted him to copy, say: "Can do!" and return one week later for a fitting. One fitting was usually all it took.

Once, on a special occasion I did buy an embroidered white blouse at Yates Road (Tongfu Lu today). Yates Road was named after an American Southern Baptist missionary who had published a grammar of Shanghai dialect in 1847. Yates Road was lined on both sides with shop windows displaying luxurious hand-embroidered lingerie and blouses. Some of these items made of heavy satin, georgette or crepe de Chine were actually sold at highly inflated prices in boutiques on Rue de la Paix in Paris, France. In Shanghai, such underwear could be bought very cheap. In fact, American ladies complained that when they gave their Shanghai purchased nightgowns to dry clean in the States, the cost of the cleaning was well above the price for which they had purchased the item. Americans were also very fond of mandarin coats sold on Yates Road which they used for evening wear.

I was puzzled by my tailor Wu, but I did like him. Other women would get into big arguments with their tailors, who usually stood their ground. One Englishwoman told my mother about the constant argument with her tailor about the length of her dresses. He insisted her dresses reach only as far as her knees—which was the style at the time—but she commanded him to make them longer. After each fitting, she would demand he lengthen the skirt, and he would return for yet another fitting with the very same skirt pretending he had lengthened it! Finally, she gave up arguing, since his clothes fit so well and were so elegant.

A Russian lady told my mother how she had once ordered a fancy dress for Easter by showing her Chinese tailor a pattern. "Makee same same" (make it exactly the same), she told him. He did so: the dress was indeed a perfect copy with the skirt carefully hand embroidered: Vogue Pattern 101!

I don't know where my father got his clothes. No men's tailor ever visited our home. Possibly, he patronized, as they called them then, a "Gents Tailor." There were many scattered around the International Settlement and the French Concession: Best Brothers, Wei Lee, Heng Kong and others.

However, there was one man in Shanghai who NEVER ordered suits from a Chinese tailor. He was "Big Ears Du," the terrifying leader of the underworld based in the French Concession. Du Yue-Sheng was born in a poor village in Pootung (Pudong) in 1887. From his early youth he was a tough hooligan and soon joined the infamous Green Gang. Later, when he became very powerful and rich, he bought a mansion not too far from my home in the

Left: Author at age 16, 1939.
Right: Piano teacher's concert, 1941. Author standing extreme right of the second line.

French Concession. Today it is the Donghu Hotel. I never knew who lived there but always wondered why the walls surrounding it were so high, with sharp pieces of glass all over the top to prevent people from sneaking into the property. Besides, several men stood on the roof visibly carrying guns. I thought a Chinese millionaire lived in the huge villa since I knew nothing about gangsters.

As far as Du's personal life was concerned, it was said he had four wives and innumerable concubines. Big Ears had one personal fear: Chinese tailors. One day, so the story went, Du visited a fortune-teller who warned him that he would have to be very careful which tailors he used. In addition, the man solemnly warned him, monkeys' heads would protect him from a violent death. Du was superstitious and strongly believed in dangerous omens. After his session with the fortune-teller, he began to patronize an excellent English tailor, Charles Norman Gray, who had arrived in Shanghai in 1912 and opened a very successful tailoring company on Nanking Road In addition to his tailoring job, Du often asked Gray to travel to Singapore to buy monkeys' heads for him. Trust a Chinese tailor? Never! Who could guarantee that during a fitting the tailor (secretly paid off by a rival gang) would not suddenly grab a knife hidden in his gown and stab Big Ears to death? Du was always extremely polite to Gray and paid him exorbitantly for his trips in search of monkeys' heads. Apparently, the fortune-teller was right: Du Yue-Sheng died a peaceful death in his own bed in 1951.

Chapter 7

BROADCASTING

Radio stations in Old Shanghai broadcasted in various foreign languages: English, French, Russian and German. The pioneer in commercial radio was XMHA, the favorite of most English speaking residents. When I was very young, my friends and I listened daily to its children's program. Its opening music was *The Teddy Bear's Picnic*. Our hearts tightened with excitement when we heard the first lines of the song:

"If you go out in the woods today,
You'd better not go alone…"

A man with a very pleasant voice who called himself "Uncle John" then continued the program with stories, songs and jokes. A memorable day for many children was when Uncle John invited them to come to a local cinema in the French Concession. A microphone had been set up there and children could recite a poem or sing a song for all to hear. Every volunteer would also get in return, an "Eskimo Pie" (a small block of chocolate coated vanilla ice-cream).

After much pleading on my part, my mother took me there. I stared at hordes of over-excited kids. When it was my turn to approach the mike, the poem I had intended to declaim (I had no voice and did not dare to sing!) vanished from my memory. Blushing and stammering, all I could manage was: "Hello mama and papa. I am talking on the radio." Still, I did get the Eskimo pie!

On June 16, 1938, an American journalist, Caroll Alcott joined XMHA for a part-time job, and became so successful that he soon started broadcasting

Selling newspaper.

every day, seven days a week. As the Japanese penetrated more and more deeply into China, telephone lines were often cut off, the cable company disrupted and XMHA became a means for missionaries, businessmen and diplomats to communicate with their representatives in the interior of China.

The Japanese began infiltrating all of Shanghai, from the area north of the International Settlement (Hongkou). They penetrated more and more deeply towards the French Concession with slogans such as "Asia for the Asians" and "the building of a 'Co-Prosperity' sphere for Asians." As Alcott became more and more critical of their bullying tactics, a delegation of Japanese visited him demanding that he say "something nice" about the Japanese army. The American promised to do so and in his next broadcast Alcott informed listeners (which included many English speaking Chinese) of his promise. He added that he would indeed keep his word should the actions of the Japanese military warrant praise.

Alcott suggested that they start by closing the opium dens that had sprung up in sections the Japanese occupied, end kidnappings and terror, and stop paying poor Chinese peasants for their produce with worthless military yen. After this broadcast, the Japanese bombed XMHA—fortunately causing little damage—and Alcott had to hire bodyguards for protection.

Alcott organized the first fully sponsored news broadcasts in China helping XMHA make much money. He often started his program announcing: "Jell-o! Jell-o! Jell-o!" (Jelly crystals to which one simply added hot water to make a dessert). He also sponsored other products including Bakerite Bread, Maxwell House Coffee, and Ovaltine. Alcott sympathized very much with the suffering of the poor in China. As he walked the streets, he was shocked that in spite of prosperous international and Chinese companies, many residents suffered terrible hunger. He described how once when he strolled along the Bund, he noticed a Chinese woman at the end of a jetty washing something long and sticky. As he came nearer, he realized that she was cleaning her dinner: noodles covered with filth. An English policeman was standing near by and when Alcott asked him if the woman did this often, the policeman explained:

"She does it every day. That's the way she lives. What she doesn't eat she sells to urchins for a few coppers. Often noodle hawkers serving customers drop some noodles on the street. The noodles get filthy when people step on them, and wheelbarrows, rickshaws, and bicycles run over them. This woman eats what she can get."

Another time, Alcott observed a large number of coolies working very hard to sink an 80 ft. raft for the construction of a new building. The man in charge of the work was Chinese but had been educated in one of the Shanghai British schools, so he spoke English very well. When Alcott asked him why he did not use electric power to do the work, the man replied:

"And what would I do with my men? Let them and their families go hungry?"

As World War II broke out in Europe, Shanghai became the radio propaganda center of the Far East. Alcott began calling Japan's New Order, the New Odor. Besides XMHA, the British station XCDN broadcast programs in a dozen languages. The German station XGRS heavily pushed Fascist propaganda.

Before Pearl Harbor, Alcott left Shanghai for Manila on vacation. He sailed on the *President Harrison*. It was the *Harrison's* last crossing. On its return trip to Shanghai, the vessel was seized by the Japanese. Alcott could no longer go back to Shanghai.

Snack bar in the street and a poor woman collecting waste, painted by Austrian artist Friedrich Schiff.

Those of us who knew Russian could listen throughout the Japanese occupation to Russian broadcasts since the Soviet Union was not at war with Japan. While all "enemy nationals," Americans, British, Dutch, were imprisoned in Japanese camps, only pro-Axis stations were allowed to function. Russian news went from mouth to mouth and most other foreigners could somehow learn the actual political situation through the "Bamboo Wire" (whispered news from ear to ear). In fact, the Russians published a daily leaflet in Russian, distributed by a bearded, disheveled man who ran through the French Concession shouting headlines.

Yes, since complicated politics bubbled over and over in Old Shanghai, Old China Hands never appeared to have problems readjusting to other countries. Many spoke a variety of languages and were used to mingling with nationals from almost all countries in the world. Many became very successful when they immigrated to new countries, as did Chinese Shanghailanders.

Chapter 8

BLUE CAPS

One Friday evening as we sat at the dinner table, my father told us that a small number of Chinese Jews, from Kaifeng in Henan Province, now lived in Shanghai. The day before, my father had met a prominent businessman who told him that his clerk was a descendant of Jews who had settled in Kaifeng in the 12th century. The clerk looked like any other Chinese man—no Jewish features could be discerned in his face. After talking to him, my father found out that he could recite by heart several passages of the Hebrew Bible and that, for generations, nobody in his family ever ate pork, which is forbidden to Jews. The clerk also informed him that Jews in Kaifeng wore blue skull caps to differ them from Moslems who wore white ones. Many people simply referred to them as "Blue Caps."

"I remember that many years ago," continued my father, "a Kaifeng Jew arrived in Shanghai with his son—then a little boy—and had his child circumcised. About a decade later, the father died and the boy remained. When his father was buried in a local Jewish cemetery, his son declared that he would return to Kaifeng when he became old and be buried among other members of his family who had passed away. To everyone's surprise, he did indeed keep his word and when he reached the age of 60, in spite of many difficulties, he made his way back to the city where he was born."

My mother then added that several years ago, when she went to buy flowers for Pesach (Jewish Easter) on Route des Soeurs (Ruijin Yi Lu today), she was disappointed that her favorite little French Concession flower shop was closed. She later discovered that this particular store was owned by a Chinese from Kaifeng, who claimed he was Jewish. He observed all important Jewish holidays by shutting his business.

Kaifeng Jews were of Middle Eastern origin, most probably from Persia (Iran). They arrived in China in the early 12th century, traveling by caravan to the Song Dynasty (960–1279) capital of China. At the time, Kaifeng was the great cultural center of North China, a beautiful city with tree-lined avenues, gorgeous palaces and gardens, and a focal point for trade contacts not only with all of China, but with many nations of the outside world. A scroll treasured by the Chinese, the Qing Ming Shang He Tu (*Pure Brightness Day on the River*), painted by a famous artist Zhang Zeduan (1085–1145) around the time of the Jews' arrival, can still be seen at a famous Beijing Palace Museum. Middle Eastern Jews had been engaged for many centuries in trade with the Chinese and always had good relations with them. Persian (Iranian) Jews were much admired in China for their remarkable cotton cloth, its weaving, dyeing and design.

When the caravan of Jews arrived in Kaifeng intending to settle permanently there, they were graciously received by the heartwarming words of the Song Emperor:

"Respect and preserve the customs of your ancestors."

The Jews promised that they would teach the Chinese all they knew about cotton manufacture, and they kept their word. They became very loyal Chinese citizens.

In 1163, Jews were permitted to build a synagogue on a street named "Teaching the Scriptures Lane." The synagogue was erected in a rectangular, walled compound, directed to the West (towards Jerusalem) which the Jews faced during their prayers. The architecture was Chinese but there could be no doubt that it was indeed a Jewish synagogue: the Ark of the Covenant (an important part of each synagogue which Jews first constructed in Biblical times during their wanderings in the desert after their escape from Egypt) held beautiful *Torah* (first division of the Jewish *Bible*, the *Five Books of Moses*) scrolls in gilded containers, and wooden boxes with treasured Hebrew texts.

As in all temples in China, the synagogue displayed a tablet in praise of the emperor, which was set on a table.

Kaifeng Jews practiced circumcision, observed Shabbath (Saturday, the

A Jewish man in Kaifeng, 1908.

holy day of rest) and major Jewish feasts, read the *Torah* and other holy Hebrew texts, and prayed. The synagogue was open every day. The first Rabbi in Kaifeng was called in Chinese Li Wei, probably originating from the Jewish name Levy.

In the 15th and 16th centuries, traffic on the Silk Road declined after a new sea route from Europe to the Far East was opened on May 17, 1498 by the Portuguese seafarer, Vasco da Gama (1469–1524). Voyage by sea was safer and cheaper than overland: no taxes, no restrictions, no sudden enemy attacks. This led to the growing isolation of scattered Jewish communities in China. In time, only the one in Kaifeng survived.

How did historians piece together the history of Jews in Kaifeng? From various sources, Chinese gazetteers, Christian visitors and writers and travelers' tales, this history is preserved until today. Two inscribed stones (stelae) had been placed in the courtyard of the Kaifeng synagogue, protected by a pavilion.

The two stones, placed back to back and held tightly together by iron bands, are dated 1489 and 1512. Both stones stand 5 meters high. Their two visible surfaces had been polished smooth, and carved with Chinese characters. Today, the 1489 and 1512 stones are preserved in the Kaifeng Municipal Museum.

The 1489 stone relates that a group of 17 clans arrived in Kaifeng early in the 12th century, bearing a tribute of cloth for the emperor. Their religion was called "The Religion that plucks the sinews" (this refers to the preparation of kosher meat). The inscriptions tell about Judaism as well as the story of Abraham and memorialize the names of prominent Chinese Jews who contributed to the reconstruction of their Synagogue after a destructive flood in 1461. Renewed Yellow River floods were often catastrophic in Kaifeng.

There is also 1663 stone, which has disappeared, but here once again Shanghai comes into the picture. Shanghai Jesuits who traveled to Kaifeng in the 18th century made rubbings of its inscriptions, brought them back to Shanghai where they were eventually preserved at the Siccawei Jesuit Mission. It tells the story of yet another disastrous flood in Kaifeng (1642), which severely damaged the temple and its scriptures, and the renewed reconstruction efforts.

In 1601 Father Matteo Ricci (1552–1610), who had traveled from Rome to

China, met for the first time a Chinese Jew. Propelled by the possibility of finding as yet undiscovered ancient Christian documents, Ricci sent Rome a detailed report about his encounter with a Chinese Jew. This was how, eventually, the Western world learned the sensational news of the existence of some estimated 1,000 Jews in Kaifeng.

One of the most interesting items written in Kaifeng between 1660–1670, was the Codex —a registration of Jews in Kaifeng, the only existing ancient document in both Chinese and Hebrew. It is a 109 page long list of 453 men and 259 women. It appears that non-Jewish women were sometimes integrated within the community either by marriage or by adoption. This was classified as "adding new relatives." No names nor number of children are given. At the time when the Codex was written, only 7 of the original Jewish clan names remained. Actually, since there were 2 different clans named Li, in Kaifeng, Chinese commonly referred to the Jews as "the 8 clans with 7 names." The original Codex is at present at the Jesuit Institute in Rome.

In 1800 the last Jewish Rabbi in Kaifeng died, the Jews had no longer a teacher, and gradually the Kaifeng Jewish community became isolated. As centuries passed, the Jews became culturally assimilated with the Chinese majority, educated men passed civil examinations and obtained high government positions. They were very dedicated Chinese citizens. Most Jewish men married Chinese women and eventually their children became indistinguishable from other Chinese. Gradually fewer and fewer Kaifeng Jews could read Hebrew and only remembered the elementary precepts of Judaism. They wore traditional Chinese clothes, spoke and wrote in the local dialect and prided themselves on their elegant pigtails. By 1900 Kaifeng had lost some of its glamour having suffered treacherous floods and war. The situation of many of its citizens—including Jews—became rather desperate.

Now, Shanghai came back into the picture. News of the disintegration of the Kaifeng Jewish community reached Middle Eastern Jews who had settled in Shanghai. They felt a particular closeness to Chinese Jews who had also originated in the Middle East.

At the beginning of the 20th century, a group of Shanghai Middle Eastern Jews sent a Chinese envoy to Kaifeng. His job: to study the true situation of the Blue Caps and return to Shanghai with a full report. Upon arrival in Kaifeng, the envoy was to deliver to the Kaifeng Jews a letter from their

Shanghai co-religionists. This letter was written in Hebrew and signed by 44 local Shanghai Jews. It was addressed to their "brethren in faith." The missive stated in part:

... sorrow and anxiety filled our hearts when we read those evil tidings...All that you may require we will endeavor to supply you with, for there are in this city men of our faith... who can help you to maintain yourselves and your sons and daughters...

When the envoy returned months and months later, the envoy reported that there were only 99 Chinese of Jewish descent in Kaifeng. Transportation to and from Kaifeng was very difficult and dangerous. Bandits often attacked travelers, robbing—and sometimes murdering—them. Roads were in very bad condition, often non-existent. Inns outside of the main cities were disreputable: there was no running water, no heat and numerous bedbugs!

This news was very discouraging to Shanghailanders. Although they organized a society to aid Kaifeng Jews, mainly led by the well-known Sopher family, they made very little headway. Besides, Japanese were infiltrating Shanghai deeper and deeper in the so-called "Undeclared War," to which Japan always referred to as "incidents," and the Shanghai Jewish Community was already becoming overburdened with refugees in desperate need of immediate help: penniless Russians fleeing starvation and anti-Semitism in their country, Middle Eastern Jews arriving because of anti-Semitism in their homeland, followed by European Jews escaping the Holocaust. Till the beginning of the Pacific War after the Japanese bombing of Pearl Harbor in 1941, Shanghai was the only city in the world that kept its doors open and its hands outstretched in help.

What is the situation of Jewish descendants in Kaifeng today?

In 1985, a group of American Jews met at Stanford University to found the Sino-Judaic Institute. The main focus of their discussions was Kaifeng and its remaining Jewish descendants, as well as cultural understanding and exchange between the Jewish people and the Chinese people. I am a member of their Board. A few years ago, the SJI sent to the city of Kaifeng a permanent exhibit on the ancient Chinese Jewish community. Chinese and English texts accompanied the exhibit's maps, drawings and photographs. This exhibit is now open to the public. The Institute also organized a traveling exhibit, which it loans to museums throughout the United States and other interested countries.

How many Jewish descendants are there in Kaifeng today? This is the subject of controversy. Some estimate their number to be 1,000 or more but, it appears, 200 Chinese can be more readily classified as being Jewish. Many Jewish tourists from all over the world travel from Shanghai, Nanjing and Beijing to Kaifeng to keep in touch with descendants of Chinese Jews. Shanghai and Kaifeng are becoming linked closer and closer together.

The history of Kaifeng Jews reflects the courage and perseverance of a small group of Jews in their efforts to preserve their heritage in the face of great odds. When floods destroyed their synagogue again and again, the

Shanghai Jewish Refugees Memorial.

Jews rebuilt it. When rebellions and wars disrupted their lives, they restarted all over again. Finally, centuries of struggle and isolation from the Jews in the rest of the world led to their doom. The story of Chinese Jews is also the story of Chinese tolerance, their welcome to Jewish traders, and their good relations with them throughout many centuries.

I had a pleasure to meet Shi Lei, a Kaifeng Jewish descendent who studied Judaism at the Bar Ilan University in Israel. Regarding Kaifeng, he stated in one of his writings:

...There is nothing left, no Synagogue, no heritage, only the memory of our ancestry...Visits to Kaifeng by Jews living in various parts of the world are really helpful to Jewish descendants there, because they help us learn more about our past.

And that past will never die.

Chapter 9

MONEY, BANK AND A TYCOON

When I was growing up, Chinese currency divided into "big" and "small" money according to value. Since I never had money, I did not worry about the complicated currency system. However, foreigners eventually grew used to it and, with the happy-go-lucky Shanghai *maskee* attitude, shrugged their shoulders and accepted it.

The Chinese silver dollar, which people called "Mexican Dollar," was referred to as "Big Money." At the time, the Mexican Dollar was worth more than US $1.00.

The decimal system was followed. 10, 20 and 50 cent silver coins, or sometimes notes (Small Money) could be added together and converted into "Big Money." Bank notes were for l, 10, 100 dollars. 1 dollar was usually worth 300 coppers. Coppers could also be exchanged into cash: 3,000 to $l! I must admit I never was given this type of "cash" —which I found cute— small, round copper circles with square hole in the middle, carried with string pulled through the holes, and tied together in a knot. Occasionally, cash consisted of pyramid shaped silver paper, carried on a bamboo stick by the Chinese. All these currencies were used throughout China.

"Taels" were used for major commercial transactions. They were made of silver, shaped somewhat like a shoe, weighing about one ounce, with slight weight differences in various localities. The most common government measure of the tael was the "Treasury Tael" (*Kuping*) weighing about 37.3 grams. Another tael (*Caoping*) weighed slightly less—36.7 grams, but the silver used to make it was less pure. In traditional Chinese funerals, silver paper taels were an important item that accompanied burials so as to enable the deceased to satisfy his or her needs in the "other world." On March 1, 1933, the national Chinese Central Bank decided to simplify and standardize currency throughout China.

The entire money situation did not affect me as a child. The most money I was ever given was 2 dollars when I went to a movie: 60 cents for an entrance ticket, 40 cents for ice cream or popcorn and some cents for public transportation (tram or bus). I always returned to my parents whatever money was left over.

When I was young, what really excited me was a trip to the Bund, and I loved to stare at the line of amazing buildings, mostly banks symbolizing foreign wealth and power (a fact of which I was, of course, unaware at the time). Most great banks lined the avenue facing the Whangpoo River. I loved the teeming life on the Bund, the coolies chanting as they dragged heavy burdens, the wheelbarrows, the rickshaws darting in and out among the cars and other motored vehicles—which were very few in numbers compared to today. The Whangpoo itself appeared just as busy, with huge junks, sampans and sometimes ships of war.

Foreign banks on the Bund, or its cross roads, belonged to various proud foreign nationalities: French, Belgian, British, American, German, Italian and Dutch. Several large Chinese banks built in "modern style" also stood alongside. I used to open my eyes wide to stare at the majestic constructions, and craned my neck to glance at their roofs with the flags that sometimes adorned them.

The most exciting bank, in my opinion, was the British Hong Kong and Shanghai Banking Co., Ltd. with its magnificent bronze lions representing Great Britain's "unconquerable" might. The bank had ordered two bronze lions in England, imported them and placed outside its front entrance according to the laws of *feng shui*. The lion with his mouth firmly closed, was named Stitt, after the British Hong Kong and Shanghai Bank's British manager, G.H. Stitt. The lion with the open mouth was named Stephen, after the British manager of the Hong Kong Branch office—A.G. Stephen.

Why did one lion have a closed mouth, while the other's was shut? Here is the story my amah once told me. At first, the Shanghai Stitt lion arrived with an open mouth. But, oh danger! This would allow him to breathe in the dangerous Eastern wind at night (because of the direction in which he was placed) and he would come to life—a formidable menace to everyone on the Bund! According to amah, in order to avoid this tragedy, his head was sculptured once again, this time with his mouth firmly shut.

The lions had been created by an English sculptor named W.W. Wagstaff and poured by a Chinese artist: Chou Yin Hsing. In 1935, a copy of these two lions was placed in front of the new Hong Kong and Shanghai Bank building in Hong Kong.

When I was a little girl and my parents took me to the Bund, my father would lift me up close towards a bronze lion at the entrance the Hong Kong and Shanghai Bank. Happily, I would pat his imperial looking head but really wanted to kiss him! However, I did not dare do so. I knew my father would get angry and start telling me about nasty germs. Superstitious Chinese also patted the lions as they passed by, hoping some of the power and wealth they

The bronze lion in front of the British Hong Kong and Shanghai Banking Co., Ltd.

represented would rub off on them!

During the Pacific War, when the Japanese occupied Hong Kong in 1943, it was rumored that they had decided to transfer the lions to Japan. People whispered that they had transported the lions to Yokohama in addition to several other bronze statues erected in Hong Kong glorifying England's history. Most Shanghailanders suspected that the Japanese might melt down the lions and use the bronze for military purposes, but they were wrong. After the war, when some American occupation forces entered Hong Kong, they discovered the missing Hong Kong lions. The Shanghai lions had remained in Shanghai.

When the "cultural revolution"(1966–1976) erupted throughout China, the Shanghai Artifact Administration Board moved the lions to be stored in the warehouse of the Shanghai Comedy Troupe. In 1980, they were handed over to the Shanghai Museum. 17 years later, the Pudong Development Bank moved into the former Hong Kong and Shanghai Bank building and a copy of the original lions was placed in front of the entrance once again.

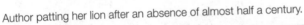

Author patting her lion after an absence of almost half a century.

One of the first things I did when I returned to Shanghai for the first time after an absence of almost half a century, was to go to the Bund and pat "my lions" that I had never forgotten!!!

Before powerful banks came into play, how did the Chinese exchange money? As Shanghai boomed into a big trade and business center, money exchange stores sprang up all over the city. In fact, they existed throughout my youth and were widely used.

When I grew older, I found out there were different levels of money exchange stores:

The biggest ones, *Hwei Hwa*, were really Chinese banks. Their owners were members of the Shanghai Money Exchange Merchants' Association.

The group below them, *Tiao Ta*, was not Association members but their business was similar to that of banks: savings, current accounts and trusts.

The third class exchange shops had sprung up all over Shanghai, both in the International Settlement and in the French Concession, in small lanes and on corners of main streets. I remember them clearly. They had signs in English stating "Money Exchange" and colorful—usually white and red—flags with Chinese characters. Surprisingly to me, they also sold cigarettes and sweets. In addition, many had a special service for illiterate Chinese: a man who read and wrote letters for a fee.

All these dingy little stores were reputed to be honest and reliable according to old Chinese tradition, and their exchange rates were usually more favorable than those of banks.

Talking of Chinese money, one remarkable story that perplexed all Shanghai was that when a foreign tycoon, Silas Hardoon died, he was given a Chinese funeral, including silver paper taels! Everyone in Shanghai was familiar with Hardoon Road (Tongren Lu today), but a Chinese funeral and paper taels?

Today, the enormous Hardoon Estate is the site of the Shanghai Exhibition Center. Silas Hardoon was an Iraqi Jew who arrived in Shanghai in 1873 to work for the Sassoon Company. Unlike most other foreigners he learned the Shanghai Chinese dialect as quickly as he could and followed a friend's advice to buy plots of land—which were selling at ridiculously low prices—as soon as possible before a real estate boom developed. Hardoon earned a small salary at the time, but saved every penny he could and eventually bought

Silas Hardoon, the richest man east of Suez.

properties, which he rented out. By 1920, he was engaged in large-scale real estate speculation and became, according to an English journalist of the time, "the richest man East of Suez."

Hardoon eventually married a Chinese woman, a staunch Buddhist. Her origin remains unclear. Some say she was a Chinese seamstress, others claim her father was a Shanghai Irish policeman. They were married at the British Consulate, since Hardoon had arrived from India, a British colony and carried a British colonial passport. He called his wife Liza. She was deeply influenced by a Buddhist monk who lived on the Hardoon estate, and persuaded her to publish 8,416 rolls of Buddhist canons. The erudite monk himself personally edited this challenging material.

Since the Hardoons had no children, they adopted 11 children of European or Eurasian descent, who were brought up as Jews. All the Hardoon children wore traditional Chinese clothes at home and ate Chinese food. However, they always appeared in Western clothing outside their estate and attended Western schools. My cousin went to school with two of the Hardoon Jewish girls with whom she is in contact till today.

Most school kids walked to school or used public transportation, but the Hardoon girls' daily arrival and departure were dramatic. A uniformed chauffeur drove the girls to the school gate in a huge maroon colored Rolls Royce. The chauffeur sat in front, separated from the children, like a stagecoach driver. Sitting at his side, was another Chinese employee, whose sole function was to open the doors to let the girls step out or in. When it rained hard, an awning protected the driver and his companion.

The Hardoons also took in over 100 Chinese foster children, who all studied in a specially built Chinese school on the estate grounds. They strictly followed Chinese customs and ethics.

In 1927, Hardoon built a synagogue named "Bet Aharon." He became the only councilor both on the Board of the International Settlement Council and that of the French Concession. In 1920, the Chinese government awarded him the "Grand Ribbon Second Grade," for his various contributions to Chinese organizations, such as the "Association for Old Men" and the "Literary Society." Actually, Hardoon himself supported entirely the "Literary Society." In times of famine, Hardoon contributed millions and received yet another honor, the "Military Order of the First Class" with Sash.

My father told me that Hardoon undertook a special project—the translation into Chinese of sacred scriptures of Judaism, Christianity and Islam. Three volumes were eventually published and were distributed free of charge to educational institutions.

However, there was an unpleasant side to Hardoon's character. In spite of all his fabulous wealth, he would personally visit Chinese tenements to ensure that rent had been paid. This resulted in such bitter hatred from many Chinese that, for his safety, he had to be accompanied by a Chinese guard.

When Hardoon died in 1931, his wife Liza declared that her husband had instructed her to have two types of funerals for him: the first one Chinese, according to Buddhist rites, and the second Jewish. A young friend of mine told me that he was taken by his father to attend both funerals. The Chinese funeral procession was led to the burial site on the estate grounds, by two bands: one band played traditional Chinese music, and a second band followed with military marches. Included in the procession were bearers of remarkable copies of all that Hardoon might need in his further life, including silver paper taels. Later, Hardoon lay in state while thousands of joss sticks (incense) glowed at his sides. His Chinese foster children kowtowed respectfully in front of their father's body.

A Jewish funeral followed the Chinese funeral, which infuriated the president of the Jewish Burial Society since he had been misled into believing that only Jewish services would be held.

Thus Hardoon was buried in controversial circumstances. He left the bulk of his fortune to his wife, Liza. Litigation about his will continued until Mrs. Hardoon's death in 1941.

Chapter 10

THE TRIUMPH OF JESSE OWENS

Fascism in Europe created great anxiety among the foreign population of Shanghai, as well as among a great number of Chinese. Before the rising power of Hitler, Berlin had been chosen as the site for the 1936 Olympic Games and this fact could no longer be changed. Now, the increasing power of Nazis and their aggressive behavior began to worry the rest of the world. For Hitler, it was a perfect opportunity to show the entire world the power of the "Master Race," to which Germans claimed to belong.

Propaganda Minister Joseph Goebbels was delighted. What a great opportunity for him to show 49 competing countries the superiority of Germans! Didn't the Nazis have a superstar athlete Lutz Lang who was blond and blue-eyed—a real Aryan?

At the French Municipal College that I attended at the time (I was 13 years old then), pupils kept talking about the "horrible Boches" (disparaging term in French for Germans). Marie, my French classmate shouted passionately:

"Quoi? Eux superieurs? Nous avons la meilleure armee du monde! La Grande Guerre (1914–1918) l'a certainement demontre!!"

(What? They are superior? We have the best army in the world! The Great War (1914–1918) has certainly proved this.)

The Germans had completed their impressive Olympic stadium for 100,000 spectators with German punctuality. They also made a point of hiding their fiercely anti-Semitic policy: no anti-Semitic posters, no signs stating "Jews not

Cinema in Old Shanghai.

admitted" were anywhere to be seen. But, once the Games started, there was no way to hide Jesse Owens' amazing performance, nor that of other Black American participants.

When we, in Shanghai, read that Jesse Owens had won the first Gold Medal for the 100m Race, thousands of young and old people in Shanghai cheered and celebrated. Hitler had refused to personally place the gold medal around the winner's neck. It was said that in a fit of fury, Hitler also declared that the Americans should be ashamed for having sent a black man to represent their country. According to Nazi ideology, an African or Asian was automatically inferior to any pure white Aryan man.

The Nazis were bitterly disappointed when Jesse Owens went on to win gold medals for the 200m Race, the Long Jump and the 4 x100m Relay Race. He broke 11 Olympic records and defeated blond blue-eyed Aryan Lutz Lang in a very close Long Jump final.

Besides Jesse, there were ten other African American members in the team of American athletes. Between them they won 7 gold medals, 3 silvers and 3 bronzes at the Berlin Olympics.

But joy in Shanghai, and probably many other parts of the world did not last long. Hitler continued occupying country after country in Europe, while the Japanese pursued their aim of dominating a great part of Asia. They soon took over Shanghai completely and ruled with a tough fist.

A few years later, in order to promote the might of the Axis powers, the Japanese announced they would be showing a documentary of the Berlin Olympics in a theater in the French Concession. The cinema sold out all tickets immediately, but the Japanese failed to understand the reason for this success. My friends and I, as well as other foreigners and Chinese both young and old, thronged to see the Olympics documentary. Here was an opportunity to watch a film openly showing the Stars and Stripes fluttering on the screen, as well as athletic triumphant Americans entirely different from those in present-time newsreels—haggard, starving Allied prisoners being led to some distant concentration camp.

When Jesse Owens appeared on the screen, there were loud shouts of "Bravo!" Later, my friends and I worried the Japanese would become aware of the strong anti-Japanese reaction but, remarkably, they did not perceive the true reason for the loud cheers. Actually, I saw the film three times and clapped so hard that the palms of my hands ached!

The Japanese occupiers completely misinterpreted the enthusiastic applause in the cinema, and soon the following news was printed in one of the Shanghai English language newspapers:

SECOND OLYMPICS GAMES SHOWING AT DOUMER THEATER

Current at the Doumer Theater is the second part film record of the Olympic

Jesse Owens won 4 gold medals in the 1936 Olympic Games.

Games held in Berlin in 1936. Since the first part of the film Fest der Voelker *enjoyed a 15-day run, a rare case for a foreign film, the success if the second part is a foregone conclusion.*

Shanghai laughed and, as the film showings proceeded, continued applauding the American flags and the success of Jesse Owens!

As to Japanese Domei Agency, who could possibly take it seriously, news such as the following made Shanghai smirk:

U.S. GUNNERS SHOOT 20 OF THEIR OWN PLANES

American inefficiency is becoming clearer every day. Sergeant Fosie states that U.S. gunners shot down 20 of their own planes. He explained that the incidence is due to inexperience.

I copied out many such news reports in my diaries, which I have kept until today! Here is another report:

The American defilement of the remains of Japanese soldiers killed in action was revealed in two Domei dispatches from Zurich and was bitterly assailed by the Yomiuri-Hochi Shimbun *in its editorial this morning. One of the dispatches reported that in the United States children were found playing with the skulls of Japanese soldiers killed in action, which American soldiers on the Pacific front had sent home as "souvenirs."*

The *Yomiuri-Hochi* further pointed out that such behavior

...should be traced to the brutal nature rooted deeply in the national character of the American people as well as to the superiority complex they maintain towards East Asiatics...

Such cases of inevitable barbarism on the part of the American army may be almost incomprehensible to the Japanese people who cherish the spirit of Bushido or Chivalry, but they reveal the true character of our enemy who talks like a gentleman but acts like a beast.

An up-to-date:

Polo Ralph Lauren is the official outfitter to the U.S. Olympic and Paralympic teams 2008. According to an Associated Press article on May 4, 2008, the inspiration for their styles came from the days of Jesse Owens, in an era before tracksuits became essentially the uniform for Olympians around the world. The designer, Ralph Lauren, said:

"We wanted to reference the glory days of the Olympics and then bring it to a very modern silhouette. It's a combination of looking back and looking to the future. The looks range from classic polo shirts with graphic Chinese lettering that read 'Beijing' to tennis and cricket sweaters paired with ties." He further added: "When an athlete wears them, the clothes truly come alive."

Chapter 11

EXPATRIATE HOUSEHOLDS—
LIFE IN PARADISE

In Shanghai, nationals of Great Powers—who would be called "expatriates" today—entered a new phase in their lives, one that they had never experienced. From the moment they arrived, their trunks were unpacked for them, their homes organized and run by efficient Chinese help. Unobtrusively, the servants rapidly set their home in order, had their clothes washed, ironed and hung up or neatly stacked in drawers, and their food professionally prepared.

Usually, the foreign men would arrive first, followed by their wives and children. Even if the man was not a top-notch director or manager in his company, his life changed radically. In his home country—if he was lucky—his wife had a cleaning woman once a week. In Shanghai, his wife hardly ever entered their kitchen, nor did she shop for food, prepare menus (except perhaps when giving a party). Neither did she wash, iron nor clean. Compared to her husband's salary, Chinese servants were extremely cheap, and, if kindly treated, extremely loyal and industrious. They provided food and clothing for themselves out of their low wages. Their employers' homes usually had special servants' quarters. However, it was a generally known fact that Chinese servants usually got "squeeze" money (a small percentage) on the side when they made purchases for their employers. Most foreigners accepted this practice and did not resent it because they were well aware of the small salaries their employees earned. Chinese servants very rarely asked for a day off, except for Chinese New Year to worship at their ancestral shrine and visit their relatives. They usually returned bearing gifts of sticky triangular rice, embedded with sweet soybeans, wrapped in bamboo leaves.

Every household seemed to be run by a "Number One Boy" (as male servants were called). He quickly learned all the preferences of his bosses, and fulfilled their wishes almost before they were uttered. He respectfully called his employers "Masta" (master) and "Missie" (mistress). In addition, there was the cook who reigned supreme in the kitchen, wash amahs, baby amahs and Number Two and Three boys to do whatever other jobs around the house were required. Additional coolies were hired when needed.

Around the world, in the 1920's and 1930's, Shanghai was referred to as the "Paris of the East," a fast growing modern metropolis where expatriates lived a dream-like existence making money and enjoying themselves. Upon arrival, the family immediately had name-cards printed. Then the man of the family would personally deposit cards in the homes of other members of his company. This was done in order to announce his arrival. Usually two cards were dropped: one for the gentleman and, if he was married, another for his wife. After that, those who had received the cards would generally phone the

Western orchestra in Old Shanghai.

A ball held by the Russian in Shanghai, 1934.

newcomers and extend invitations for tea or dinner. When invited to a formal dinner party, the men would usually wear dark elegant suits and the women long dresses. At official dinner parties, men would arrive in tuxedos.

Foreigners also frequented the thousands of nightclubs, cabarets and bars scattered in the International Settlement and French Concession. A favorite saying was: "Lets go out and make whoopee!" People would go dancing at the Cathay and Palace Hotel, in nightclubs like Del Monte, Farren's, Ciro's (the first in Shanghai to have air conditioning), DD's and many others. DD's had a great band and was also a restaurant. As a teenager I went there and sat downstairs (the nightclub was on the second floor) to eat their indescribably delicious mango ice-cream.

Shanghai also claimed it had the "longest bar in the world" measuring 110.7 ft. and designed in English Renaissance style. Actually, this spot functioned like a businessmen's club for foreigners, and was very popular with men of all nationalities. During office lunch breaks, usually from 12:00 noon to1:30 p.m., one really had to crane one's neck to see the bar. It was completely hidden by a wall of suited men drinking cocktails and chatting!

And then, there was the infamous "Blood Alley" at the border of the French Concession and the International Settlement. During the day, "Blood Alley" was just a dull road with closed businesses but, at night, it woke up, and how! French Annamite policemen patrolled it stopping drunken fights. This was not, as one would say at the time, a "swanky" entertainment place, but businessmen did go there for excitement, although the main patrons were foreign sailors.

Shanghai children of fun loving foreigners saw little of their parents. The women joined clubs, played cards, went to tea parties dressed in floating dresses and fancy hats, while the men participated in paper hunts, various sports and frequented entertainment spots. As a result, children became very attached to their amahs whom they adored and who were utterly devoted to them. Sometimes, the mothers would become jealous of their children's love for their amahs, but—alas—not enough to dedicate more time and attention to their offspring. When English children were eventually sent back to Boarding School in England, usually at the age of 8, they often missed their amahs more than their parents.

The lives of stateless Russians, Jews, Portuguese originating in Macao, and poorer Middle Easterners were quite different. In fact, Russians used to refer to nationals of the Great Powers as *inostrantsti*, meaning "foreigners" in Russian. The fact is that for these immigrants, Shanghai had become a place of refuge. They strongly felt they were part of the city and did not have plans to move away. In my family, we never had more than two servants, a Chinese cook who behaved like the emperor of the kitchen and an amah —usually his intimidated wife, who washed, cleaned and served the table. Sometimes, when laundry accumulated, a "wash amah" was hired for the day. Everyone did go occasionally to a dance hall, or a cabaret, or a bar, but seldom on the scale other foreigners did. When I was older, I preferred small nightclubs on Yu Yuen Road (Yuyuan Lu today) where entertainment was provided by gypsies. I loved their husky voices, songs of longing and unrequited love. My friends and I were always short of cash. Sometimes, when we were in a group, I would volunteer to go in, explain to the owner that we had enough money only for one drink each and it had to be cheap: usually *kvass* (a Russian fermented soft drink) with a dash of Vodka. We were always welcomed because the place would come alive following our enthusiastic dancing on the tiny floor, and wild clapping after each performance. The waiters never bothered us trying to ply us with more drinks. They had all been informed of our financial situation.

Chapter 12

BLOODY SATURDAY

In 1937, most of Shanghai's 4 million inhabitants believed that their city was predestined to become a great commercial and industrial center. Didn't the enormous Yangtze River flow almost 4,000 miles from its source (in Tibet) across Asia to the Pacific serve the port of Shanghai, thus facilitating trade with the interior of China and other Asian countries? And the Pacific, didn't it open the doors to Europe and the United States?

In the early 1930's, 23,222 vessels sailed from Shanghai (a tonnage of 19,623,171), and 23,112 vessels entered Shanghai (a tonnage of 19,701,687). At the same time, industry grew by leaps and bounds: cotton mills, cotton weaving plants, silk, silk lace, flour mills, canned foods, cosmetics, candles, soap, hardware, machinery and many other factories. Yes, the people of Shanghai could not help but be proud of their city's remarkable development.

Casting an eye on all these successes, Japan, in its desire for expansion in Asia, began to consider the conquest of Shanghai as a goal of high priority. More and more Japanese settled in the northern part of Shanghai (Hongkew, Hongkou today), more and more incidents occurred between the Japanese and the Chinese. After each such occurrence, the Japanese apologized profusely for catastrophic consequences claiming it had all been a "mistake." In truth, an undeclared war was in progress between China and Japan.

Shanghailanders will never forget the disastrous day of August 14, 1937, which well deserved the name it was spontaneously given: Bloody Saturday.

My father always went to his office on Saturdays, officially for half a day, but he usually stayed longer. That August afternoon, father left his office located near the Bund to take a bus back to the French Concession, when suddenly a tremendous explosion shook the city. The bus stopped. Then came the sound of anti-aircraft guns. From where? Shanghai soon found out that it originated from the Japanese warship, *Idzumo*, firing back at a Chinese plane. The *Idzumo* was moored to the Nippon Yusen Kaisha wharf on the Whangpoo River near the Japanese Consulate and served as the Japanese Navy Headquarters. Had "real" war between China and Japan finally begun?

My father gazed in shock at blazing trams, buses and cars, and the chaos that ensued. My mother, my sister and I were away in the mountains on summer vacation, so none of this dreadful news reached us. Otherwise, I can imagine we would be sitting at home in terror waiting for my father to return.

All kinds of rumors had circulated during the previous week and Shanghai was tense expecting the Japanese to come up with yet another surprise attack. Newspapers reported that Emperor Hirohito was in continuous conference with the Japanese Army, Navy and politicians. False information circulated about the Japanese Air force having seriously wounded Generalissimo

Shanghai heavily bombed, 1937.

Chiang Kai-Shek (1887–1975) and his brother-in-law, T.V. Soong (1894–1971). Another report declared that two mail bags containing bombs about to be loaded in Hong Kong on the plane T.V. Soong was to board, exploded in his Britannic Majesty's Post Office. To my knowledge, it was never determined whether the rumor about T.V. Soong was true or false.

Apparently, previous to the explosion my father heard, several small Chinese planes flew high over Shanghai. Their plan? The Chinese had decided to take the initiative and bomb the *Idzumo*, a hated symbol of Japan's extending power over Shanghai. Originally, the *Idzumo* was a Japanese warship during the 1905 Russo-Japanese War, Japan's first victory over a major Western power. According to U.S. General C. Chennault's (1893–1958) evaluation, the Chinese airmen had been trained to bomb from 7,500 feet, but thick clouds over Shanghai forced them to come in much lower. Not being highly experienced, they probably released their bombs at 1,500 feet without adjusting their bombsights, thus missing their target.

The first bomb landed in Nanking Road between the Cathay and Palace Hotels, a part of the city always crammed with people and traffic. In the huge boom, hundreds were killed, and dismembered bodies were scattered all over the streets. One of them was a close friend of my aunt, my mother's sister. Hundreds of injured bleeding and burned people were moaning and screaming. Windows of hotels and sumptuous shops were totally blown out. The top floors of the Palace Hotel were severely damaged.

Some time later, a second devastating explosion occurred near the Race Course about a mile away. At the time, a friend of mine was riding home in a bus from down Nanking Road She later told me:

"Oh! It was so scary! The entire bus trembled and all the windows were blown out. I rushed out of the bus towards the Race Course – I don't know why in my panic I ran in the direction of the explosion instead of away from it. Stupid me! No matter how old I get I shall NEVER NEVER NEVER forget the devastation, the horror of the scene I came upon!"

What had happened? Another Chinese bomb missed hitting the *Idzumo*, and exploded in front of the Great World Amusement Center at the corner of Avenue Edward VII (Yan'an Dong Lu today, the borderline between the French Concession and the International Settlement then) and Yuyaching Road (Xizang Lu today), one of the busiest street intersections in

Shanghai.

I had always thought that the front of the Great World looked like a many-tiered wedding cake. It was the opening to an amazing labyrinth of multiple food stands, restaurants, fortunetellers, letter writers, distorting mirrors, gambling and drinking places, jugglers, musicians and theaters.

Chinese visitors loved the Great World, and foreigners who occasionally went there too, enjoyed watching happy Shanghainese laughing, having fun, drinking and eating all kinds of specialties from other provinces. After a visit to the Great World, a friend of my father's said with some surprise and admiration:

"You know, the Chinese when they are enjoying themselves and drink, appear never to reach the stage of violence and aggression as Russians often do when intoxicated. I saw no drunkards staggering around. People just appeared happy and greeted me politely. Alas, life is often so hard for the Chinese population in Shanghai. I loved watching the jolly crowds."

When the bomb crashed practically in the center of the big street crossing, it tore an enormous hole in the ground. Some newspapers reported that actually there were two bombs, a second bomb detonating a few feet away from the earth in mid air. In an instant more than 1,000 were dead, most ripped into pieces by the blast. Arms, legs, heads scattered all over the street.

The wounded screamed in agony or appeared paralysed in shock. It was indeed a scene of utter horror. Cars, rickshaws, buses were completely destroyed by flying shrapnels and burst into fire as men, women and children were burned to a cinder. Torn electric cables swung around electrocuting people.

The official Chinese statement later declared that the bomb rack in the Chinese plane had been damaged by anti-aircraft fire from the *Idzumo*, and that caused the bombs to miss their objective. Moreover, the pilot had been hit by a shrapnel just as he tried to release his bombs in the open space of the Race Course. Apparently, he finally did manage to land in Chinese territory but nobody ever confirmed to the Shanghai public whether his bomb back had indeed been damaged by the *Izumo* causing the terrible disaster.

Bloody Saturday had cost Shanghai 1,200 dead victims and 400 seriously injured men, women and children. This time, both foreigners and Chinese could not deny that the so-called "incidents" between China and Japan were

Race Course of Old Shanghai.

developing into a real war. Foreign doctors in hospitals which received the wounded testified that NOT one Chinese soldier was among the wounded. Conclusion: The statement issued by the Japanese military spokesman that those killed and wounded in the bombing were nearly all Chinese soldiers proved to be a total falsehood.

After Bloody Saturday, insecurity and panic hit Shanghai. Shopkeepers closed their stores and boarded up their fronts. People began hoarding food and money. All the big, proud banks along the Bund closed their doors. The British and Americans, as well as other European Consulates started to evacuate women and children to Hong Kong, Manila and Japan. Later, if men wished to leave too, they would also be evacuated.

Shanghai Chinese reacted with anger at what they considered "cowardly" foreign behavior. Were the foreigners now all going to run away? My father sympathized with the Chinese. He always told me:

"Don't believe a word of Japanese propaganda! According to their news reports they are always so kind and noble. No, I don't say all Japanese people are bad. In fact, I don't doubt many of them are wonderful human beings. It is their madly ambitious military forces who wish to conquer a great part of Asia, in spite of all the suffering it will cause."

Since the start of Japanese aggression in 1932, over a million Chinese refugees poured into the International Settlement and French Concession. Others left by train for Nanking and villages around the West Lake, and yet others sailed by ship to Ningpo, Canton and ports in the Southeast and the South of China.

The International Settlement and French Concession authorities did their utmost to help the crowds of refugees. Chinese guilds and the Chinese public supported them offering food and medical help. The Shanghai Waterworks and the Shanghai Power Company spared no effort to maintain their services.

After August 14, Shanghai gradually came back to life. Shops and business reopened. By the time my mother, my sister and I returned in September to our home in the French Concession, we children did not realize that Shanghai had changed in any way. Many foreigners with passports had indeed been evacuated, but all our French and stateless classmates remained, as did the families we knew.

Chapter 13

CHRISTMAS 1939

Every December 23, my sister and I awaited impatiently the arrival of gifts to our family from my father's firm, Dodwell & Co. Every year, that was the date when one of the office drivers arrived with delightful surprises and beautiful holiday greeting cards. The moment the doorbell rang, both of my sister and I would jump up and rush to the front door, too excited to wait for the amah to open it.

With a big smile on his face, the chauffeur would hand over to us a stack of bright, shiny, silver and gold paper wrapped gifts, with green mistletoe and scarlet berries displayed artistically at the corners.

Oh, lovely lovely Christmas, the jolliest holiday of the year. I was indeed a lucky Jewish girl who, besides enjoying Hannukah, celebrated Christmas with Catholic friends, Protestant friends and Greek Orthodox friends. Yes, Shanghai was indeed a melting pot and I did have a variety of great buddies.

My sister and I never opened the packages from the office before our parents' return in the evening. We kept wondering and trying to guess what treasures were in store for us. As soon as mother and father returned, we would rush to them and drag them to the bright pile of gifts. We simply could not wait another minute longer!

This year, 1939, there were big thick, illustrated volumes of *Hans Brinker or the Silver Skates* for me, and *Heidi* for my sister. Hans Brinker stood in front of a big dike, the like of which we had never seen in Shanghai, and Heidi had bright red cheeks—quite a contrast to our pale Shanghailanders' faces. My parents received their usual gifts: a bottle of Scotch whiskey for our

Street scene of Shanghai, painted by Austrian artist Friedrich Schiff.

father—which he opened sometimes when guests arrived, vodka being the preferred Russian drink—and a huge checkered tin decorated with Scottish tartan design containing Scottish shortbread for our mother. We all loved this shortbread and it might have been, in reality, the gift we had hoped for most!

To our delight, we also received an additional surprise: a big, rectangular golden box of Christmas crackers whose secrets would pour out with a big bang when my sister and I tugged at both ends and pulled them apart. As the crackers broke into two, paper hats, fake jewelry, tiny toys and miniature games would pour out. My sister and I greeted these treasures with shrieks of joy.

That was the time when Shanghailanders and Shanghainese delighted in walking on Avenue Joffre, decorated with fake pine branches. I would always stop to gaze at the festive window of my favorite Armenian bakery, *Tchakalian*. I stared at the artistically decorated *Bûches de Noël* (Christmas logs) cakes, covered with thick chocolate icing as well as edible pointy bright green holly leaves. Almost all store windows were plastered with signs saying "Joyeux Noël," or "Merry Christmas," or in Russian Cyrillic letters "Рождество!" (Christmas!). Sometimes, all three signs in different languages would be displayed in one shop, especially if it had two show-windows.

At the French Municipal College, an enormous Christmas tree reached the high ceiling of our most elegant Assembly Hall. Our school had started out as the French Club and the hall proudly displayed decorated ceilings, elegantly shaped windows, and a real stage. The Christmas tree was adorned with many colored balls and stars, flying ethereal angels, gold-painted pinecone, angel hair, and glowing multicolored electric lights. During Russian Christmas, which always came somewhat later than the Catholic and Protestant holiday (as a result of the difference in Calendars), a tall and large *Ded Moroz* (Father Christmas) stood majestically at the foot of the tree. At his side, was an enormous bag filled with little gifts for one and all. The French students did not attend the celebration of Russian Rojdjestvo at school but most Russian kids eagerly participated, be they Christian or Jewish. Usually a play was put up on the stage and songs were sung.

On Christmas Eve, I would lie in bed in the evening and imagine all the Christian children wearing their best finery praying in Catholic or Protestant churches, then returning home for a late midnight dinner of turkey, duck or fish—whatever their family tradition happened to be.

Even Chinese beggars on the streets appeared less miserable—or perhaps I imagined it. The fact is that, in the spirit of Christmas, foreigners dug more generously in their pockets to hand out money to the poor. Chinese servants, alas, got no presents. If their employers were generous, they would give them a bonus later in the year, on Chinese New year.

French Municipal College St. Charlemagne celebration, 1938. Students of various nationalities on stage. Author, third from right, second row.

As children in China, our pleasures were simple and our expectations limited, but—at least my sister and I, as well as our parents—rejoiced in joint celebrations with all citizens of all nationalities in our multi-ethnic and multi-religious, extraordinary city of Shanghai. Indeed, where else but in Shanghai, could we have freely enjoyed three Christmases, three Easters (Jewish Passover, Catholic/Protestant and Orthodox) and two great New Years: Chinese and Foreign?

Chapter 14

ABBOT CHAO-KUNG AND HIS HATRED

O ne warm Sunday, my High School classmate and I decided to go to the Public Garden, on the Bund, and have some fun. As we were walking on a path among lovely flowers, we saw coming towards us in steady stride a Chinese monk. When he approached, we realized he was not Chinese but a European. He glanced at us as he passed by giving us a piercing look through eyes that shone like black coal. When he passed, we both said:

"It's Trebitsch-Lincoln!"

To which my friend added:

"He's scary!"

Ignaz Trebitsch-Lincoln was a Jew of Hungarian origin. Later, he converted to Christianity changing several denominations, and finally he became a Chinese monk. At that point, he was given the title of "Abbot Chao-Kung" and remained a loyal Buddhist till the end of his life. He was a famous—or perhaps infamous—character in Shanghai and all over the world.

Trebitsch-Lincoln was born in a small Hungarian town, South of Budapest, Paks, in 1879. When he was a teenager, it appears he lied about his age (claiming he was older) and became a student at the Royal Hungarian Academy of Dramatic Art in Budapest. He did not complete his studies and could never hold a steady job. He was arrested for theft, and then wandered from country to country. There was no doubt that he was a highly intelligent

Author strolling on Avenue Joffre, 1940.

man, an excellent conversationalist, who had read intensively and easily picked up languages.

Trebitsch-Lincoln arrived in Shanghai in 1922. Shanghai was a city open to everyone from crooks to legitimate businessmen, from simple workers to intellectuals. It was a palette of various races, religions, nationalities and ways of life. In short, Shanghai was a perfect city for the wandering Hungarian.

Trebitsch-Lincoln was consumed by one deep hatred in his life: hatred for Great Britain because his favorite son Natzl (a pet name for Ignaz) was hanged by the English. Natzl lived in England, became a Royal Horse Artillery bombardier, and apparently had inherited some of his father's traits. When he was 20 years old, he and his army buddy broke into a home in Trowbridge (Wiltshire) with the intent of robbery. They had been drinking heavily and were intoxicated. Since neither one of the young men was accustomed to imbibe so much alcohol, it had a very negative effect on them. When the house-owner returned unexpectedly, both youngsters panicked and Natzl fired a shot that killed the man. Neighbors heard the shot, called the police, who quickly handcuffed both young men. Natzl's partner was sentenced to 14 years in prison, but Natzl was sentenced to death.

When Trebitsch-Lincoln heard of this terrible news, he immediately cabled the British authorities asking them to wait for his arrival before carrying out the sentence. He wanted to hire an expert lawyer in defense of his beloved son. His arrival, alas, would take a while because he was traveling by ship. In the meantime, he and some of his friends helped organize the collection of thousands of signatures in a plea for mercy, but the British disregarded all efforts to save Natzl. He was executed as sentenced before his father's arrival. From then on, Trebitsch-Lincoln referred to the British as cowards, hypocrites and arrogant exploiters of weaker countries. The pain and hatred resulting from his son's execution remained with him for the rest of his life.

In Shanghai, Trebitsch-Lincoln was distrusted by most people. Many accused him of being a spy for Nazi Germany because of his desire for revenge on Great Britain. His relations with the Japanese also aroused doubt and suspicion.

Shortly before I went with my friend to the Public Garden, I remember a meeting my father had with Anna Ginsbourg, a member of the editorial staff of the publication *Our Life*, of which my father was editor.

I admired Anna very much. She was an excellent reporter, enthusiastic in her beliefs and good-looking. She and my father argued often and passionately about the contents of the publication, but basically they were very good friends. When Anna told my father she wanted to interview Lincoln-Trebitz, my father erupted in anger, calling the man *podletz* (scoundrel) in Russian. My father asked her if she knew that one of his supporters was Walter Fuchs. Fuchs, a Jewish lawyer, had worked for the German Embassy, was fired and now it was rumored that he still kept contact with his former Nazi bosses, which turned him into a very suspicious character in the eyes of most Shanghailanders. Yet Anna did not give in. My good father, the idealist, who firmly believed in the freedom of the press, agreed to let her have her interview.

Anna Ginsbourg met Trebitsch-Lincoln at the Young Men's Christian

Association (Y.M.C.A.), where he lived at the time. She interviewed him downstairs where the Y. had a tea-room and restaurant. Anna called my father after the meeting and, in the evening, came over to our house glowing with excitement.

"He is a fascinating man!" she told my father, "His appearance is also most impressive. He was dressed like a real Chinese monk in a long black robe. He wore cloth Chinese shoes and no socks. Around his neck, he had a long string of beads."

Abbot Chao-Kung had created what he called the "League of Truth." He gave Anna a visiting card where it stated in French:

POUR: CONTRE:
La Verite   Le Mensonge
La Justice   L' Injustice
La Bonte   La Haine
PARTOUT ET TOUJOURS

(TRANSLATION)
FOR: AGAINST:
Truth   Lies
Justice   Injustice
Kindness   Hatred
EVERYWHERE AND ALWAYS

Abbot Chao-Kung had a devoted group of disciples. The depth of his knowledge astonished everyone. He had the ability to concentrate for long periods of time and was even able to learn the very complex Pali of Hinayana Buddhism scriptures (a small, conservative branch of the religion).

He told Anna an amazing story. He declared that he was against Zionism and had come up with the idea of settling Jews outside Shanghai on a piece of land belonging to Buddhists. It would be a model settlement. One reason he had reached this rather strange conclusion may have been Trebitsch-Lincoln's deep-rooted hatred of England. Zionism's objective was for Jews to resettle in the Land of Israel, now Palestine which was under British mandate. It must be noted that although the League of Truth proclaimed it stood against hatred, their leader had never been able to erase his deep anger against

England from his heart.

Anna's article appeared in *Our Life* on July 9, 1943. Some months later, that same year, Trebitsch-Lincoln unexpectedly died in the Shanghai General Hospital. My father's publication reported that the cause of death had been an "intestinal ailment." Trebitsch was buried in the Buddhist section of the Shanghai Municipal Cemetery. His funeral was very well attended by people of various nationalities.

Did Trebitsch-Lincoln die a natural death? Was he murdered? Had he been a spy for the Nazis against the British? These questions have not been clearly answered until this very day.

Chapter 15

THE PORTUGUESE COLONY AND FATHER ROBERT JACQUINOT DE BESANGE

In 1933, the number of Portuguese in Shanghai was officially calculated at 1,784, not a large percentage of foreigners in the enormous multi-million metropolis. This figure steadily increased to some 2,500 before the Japanese occupation of Shanghai. Some of them were Portuguese citizens, some were stateless. The majority originated in Macao and referred to themselves as Macanese. They were generations removed from Portugal, hardly knew the Portuguese language and spoke primarily a Macanese dialect, English, Shanghainese, and/or Mandarin. Their contributions in Shanghai as office workers, teachers and athletes were remarkable.

How did the Portuguese first reach the Far East and Macao?

From early days, the Portuguese were great navigators. In 1498 Vasco da Gama rounded Africa, reached India and, in 1513, Jorge Alvares was the first Portuguese to set foot on the China coast. Throughout the years, the Portuguese flew their flag in Macao and were proud of their presence on the peninsula. The Macanese were very industrious and successful tradesmen. They became wealthy but from 1700 to 1841 their fortunes declined as Britain became the world's major colonial power.

At the British Dodwell & Co. in Shanghai, a number of Portuguese

European refugees in Designated Area.

worked with my father. My father was very fond of department's Portuguese salesman and, occasionally, they would take a break and chat. My father admired the specific world outlook of the Portuguese which differed from that of most other foreigners in Shanghai and facilitated their lives. Once, after one such conversation, my father told us:

"The Portuguese in Shanghai are considered inferior by the British and other Great Powers, as are all other stateless Shanghailanders, or citizens of countries less powerful than Great Britain. The wonderful thing about them is their balanced acceptance of this situation. They know their salaries are lower than those of the British in our office, as is mine although I am the Manager of our Provision Department, but they take it in stride without agonizing. What really matters to them are their community, their family, their Catholic religion, and a pleasant way of life where good food, family entertainment and sports play a major role. They appear to be a relaxed and happy people who don't constantly struggle against the injustice of their situation."

Indeed, it seems that Portugal was different from other European countries, in that it did not discourage Portuguese voyagers from marrying native women of other lands. In Macao all their children simply became *Filhos de Macao* (sons of Macao). They had no racial prejudice at all. It was difficult to determine the exact race of the descendants of original Portuguese navigators and traders. In fact, they were a mixture of Asians (Chinese, Japanese, Burmese) and Europeans. Later, when a number of countries of the world like the United States and Australia set barriers and quotas to the immigration of Euro-Asians, the Portuguese were often included in the list.

As my father said: "Here in Shanghai, the Portuguese don't dwell on all these injustices and, on the whole they lead healthy, happy lives, enjoying numerous family gatherings, great food and sports. As you know, they are outstanding in foot-ball, tennis and swimming. They often marry among themselves and form a very united community."

At the French Municipal College in the French Concession in Shanghai, four members of the Portuguese Leitao family were the first Portuguese registered as students. The two older siblings, Manuel and Fernanda, graduated with honors, taking the newly instituted Baccalaureate essential for University admission in France and in many foreign countries. The two younger sisters, Luiza and Augusta were admired in Shanghai for their lovely singing voices. Luiza was given the title of "Deanna Durbin of Shanghai." At the time, Deanna Durbin was a very popular teen-age actress who had an extraordinary voice. In one movie, *100 Men and a Girl*, she sang with a full symphony orchestra. Manuel later studied Medicine at the Aurora University, left for Portugal and became a well-known doctor. Fernanda taught English in Shanghai, and elementary school in the United States. Many years later, I met Fernanda—who is a number of years older than I—in the United States and we became friends. Fernanda's father was highly respected in the Portuguese community. He participated eagerly in volunteer work and joined the Portuguese Company of the Shanghai Volunteer Corps, where he quickly rose in rank to Major.

Fernanda told me that the Jesuit Father, Robert Jacquinot de Besange was the Pastor of the Catholic Portuguese Community. He was the one who had baptized her, participated together with the Bishop in her Confirmation when she was 12, and conducted her marriage ceremony. She was proud of the fact that at important Portuguese celebrations, her father was always seated next to Father Jacquinot. Father Jacquinot had lost one arm and her father would cut his meat for him. Her father, in the meantime after having reached the rank of Major in Portuguese Company of the Shanghai Volunteer Corps, was put in charge of the Shanghai Rifle Range that included a Russian Regiment. Father Jacquinot was an intelligent, devout, and exceptionally courageous man who gained world renown.

Two weeks after "Bloody Saturday," the Japanese struck Shanghai wounding the British Ambassador in China who was riding in his official car with a British flag painted on its roof. Of course, as usual, the Japanese apologized after the incident, but Shanghai was stunned by their temerity. Hundreds of thousands of Chinese unable to fight back during increasing Japanese attacks started pouring into the International Settlement and the French Concession for protection. A Jesuit later wrote:

"The Garden Bridge, spanning the Suchow Creek between Chinese and Western areas, became a veritable 'Bridge of Death' where, as one observer noted, one 'walked on the bodies of Chinese children and elderly thrown to the ground.' Due to the influx of refugees, the populations of colonial Shanghai almost doubled."

At that point, Father Jacquinot took charge. He approached Chinese and Japanese authorities with a proposal: to create a "Safety Zone" of one square miles in Nantao, the old Chinese city. Since he had already been appointed President of an International Committee for Refugees and Vice-President of the local Red Cross Committee, both the Chinese and the Japanese took his proposal seriously. After three difficult days of negotiations, Father Jacquinot succeeded in his tireless efforts. The area he requested was granted to the Nantao Area Supervisory Committee. The committee was headed by Father Jacquinot. Seven other members of the Committee were foreign residents.

This safety zone, eventually dubbed "The Jacquinot Zone," finally sheltered 250,000 Chinese refugees from fighting and bombardment. The Shanghai press praised the efforts of the French Jesuit and started referring to him the "Christian Savior of Shanghai." The aim Father Jacquinot set himself: to feed and house desperate refugees.

In 1938, when Father Jacquinot traveled to the United States, President Roosevelt (1882–1945) welcomed him in the White House, praised him highly and gave him a contribution for Chinese refugees amounting to US$750,000.

Father Jacquinot had been born in 1878 in Saintes, France, into an aristocratic family. However, he always remained a deeply modest, self-sacrificing man wearing a threadbare cassock and a large blue beret. Why did he arrive in Shanghai? To study Chinese and become pastor of a Chinese Parish. He was very well-educated and taught Science at the Jesuit Aurora University which had been founded in 1913. It was at the Aurora that he lost his right forearm when a laboratory experiment failed causing an explosion. Fortunately, his eyesight was saved.

Although Father Jacquinot appeared gentle, and in truth he was a very kind man, he succeeded in life through determination, strength of character, and courage. No danger stopped him in his endeavors to save human beings. Even the Japanese were in awe of him. It is said he stopped some soldiers from committing atrocities by forcefully hitting them on the head with his wooden arm. The Protocols and Commentaries to the Geneva Convention of 1949 mentioned Father Jacquinot and the Jacquinot Zone.

Father Jacquinot remained in China for 27 years and managed to perform "miracles" in Nantao. He convinced the French authorities to supply the area with electricity and clean water, and organized a lottery that raised more than US$45,000 to help penniless, desperate Chinese refugees. The "Jacquinot Zone" was always kept remarkably clean.

After the Japanese gained more and more power in Shanghai, Father Jacquinot fought passionately to keep the neutrality of the "Zone." However, the Japanese did not comply with his proposal. They said they would assume responsibility for the area. Most refugees remained there, but soon a corrupt regime took over including organized crime and secret police. Nevertheless, Father Jacquinot never gave up. He kept helping the refugees in the Zone until the area was forcibly closed.

In the course of the Sino-Japanese war, other Chinese cities followed Father Jacquinot's example but unfortunately they were over-ruled by the occupying forces. As the Japanese advanced towards Nanking, a desperate attempt was made to create a safety zone there in the model of Father Jacquinot's in Shanghai. Alas, this endeavor was thwarted and resulted in the infamous

"Rape of Nanking."

In 1940, Father Jacquinot returned to his homeland to help war victims in suburban Paris. In 1945, he headed a Vatican delegation for refugees in Berlin. Soon after, in 1946 he died —it is said—of utter exhaustion at the age of 68.

Touching stories are told of the everlasting gratitude of humble Chinese for his love, help and self-sacrifice. He was said to have been deeply touched when a rickshaw coolie carrying him to the French Consulate, where a ceremony was about to take place awarding him the French Legion of Honor, refused to take any money from him. Instead the rickshaw man bowed respectfully and thanked him in the name of the Chinese poor.

As to former Shanghai Portuguese, Father Jacquinot's name is venerated by them until today.

Chapter 16

ALBERT EINSTEIN'S VISIT TO SHANGHAI

During the Japanese occupation of Shanghai, I lay ill in the hospital with typhoid, transmitted by a louse at one of the frequent road "barricades" imposed by Japanese soldiers when a V.I.P. (Very Important Person—at least to the occupying forces) was driven through the city. Fearing an assassination attempt, the Japanese would block certain streets, herd together beggars, farmers, students, in short all pedestrians, bicycle riders, rickshaw coolies and chauffeurs of cars. As I stood within the crowd I clearly felt a few bites on my leg. Since epidemics of various types had become more frequent, I was immediately beset by worry about the consequences. My worries were justified: I ended up hospitalized with typhoid fever at the Jewish Hospital in the French Concession.

In the hospital ward to which I was assigned, too weak even to feed myself, Zinaida Abramovna, an elderly well-educated woman, lay in a bed next to mine. She was slowly recovering from typhoid and certainly lightened my misery by telling me stories about her life and about Shanghai's past history.

"Do you know," she asked me one afternoon, "that in November 1922 Albert Einstein visited Shanghai? I was thinking of this because it is now November 1942, exactly 20 years later."

My ears pricked up. Although I had never been deeply interested in science (literature was my passion), I had admired the genius and creativity

Einstein giving a lecture.

of Albert Einstein when our teachers explained to us how he revolutionized physics.

"My late husband Sasha—may he rest in peace," Zinaida Abramovna continued, "managed to get an invitation for both of us to join a Jewish community delegation to greet Einstein on his arrival by ship. We went with a large group to a Shanghai wharf. I even remember what I wore: a small black velvet hat and an emerald green dress I had brought back to Shanghai after a trip to Paris—not that I expected Einstein to notice that! Einstein was the picture of an absent-minded professor. His hair flew untidily in the wind, but when he passed by near to me, I noticed his eyes: so kind, so gentle and so clever! Of course, a large crowd of people had gathered to greet the world famous physicist: British, American, French, various other Europeans, including stateless White Russians and hundreds of Chinese officials." She stopped, apparently reliving the scene.

"Where did he stay?" I asked, "In a hotel or in some big shot's villa?"

"Oh," she replied, "He stayed at the Astor House (Pujiang Hotel today). In the 1920's and early 1930's, the Astor House was one of the most popular hotels in Shanghai. In fact, it was the very first Western hotel in China. Many foreign celebrities stayed there including, as I remember Charlie Chaplin. The newspapers said that he remained most of the time in his room working on one of his most famous films, *City Lights*. Ah, but I am wandering away from our subject! I think Einstein hardly stayed at all in his room. He was busy,

busy all the time!"

"So," I pressed her, "what did he do?"

"Well, there were all kinds of celebrations in his honor, especially since it was in Shanghai that the Swedish Consul informed him that he had won the Swedish Nobel Prize! But, I remember, that it was only later, on July 11, 1923, that he was officially honored in Gothenburg, Sweden, in the presence of the King."

"There was such an excitement in Shanghai when we heard Einstein had received the Nobel Prize, but—as usual—he reacted with modest surprise. Every newspaper published what he said:

"'I have no special talents. I am only passionately curious.'"

Chinese cultural circles invited Einstein to a glorious welcome party, and took him to a performance of the *Kunqu* Opera. He graciously gave a lecture, which was fully attended, at the Shanghai Municipal Council on the Theory of Relativity. Long conversations and discussions with Chinese scientists followed. "And, what a lovely garden party was given in his honor by the Shanghai Jewish Community Organization! On that occasion, I wore a thin straw floppy hat and a flowered georgette dress!" Zinaida Abamovna sighed remembering her happy past, then added:

"Now, let's rest before our visitors arrive."

Some time later, her two loving daughters came and then my parents entered our ward. My mother brought two little bouquets of flowers, one for Zinaida Abramovna and one for me. While Zinaida Abramovna at once began happily chatting with her two grown girls, I recounted to my father and mother what she had told me about Einstein's visit.

"Yes," my father said. "At the time, I had been in Shanghai for only two years, struggling to survive. I read about the arrival of the great man in the papers but, of course, was not invited to attend any of the ceremonies in his honor. Later, when I met Chinese intellectuals, they often mentioned Einstein's unforgettable visit to our city and its deep influence on Chinese intelligence. Many Chinese professors and students' admiration for Einstein pushed them to dig deeper and deeper into science, especially physics. Some, after having graduated College in China proceeded to the United States to continue their studies. At that time, there was only a trickle of Chinese students who went abroad to further their studies, but Einstein's Theory of

Relativity had captured them—as it did to the entire world! "

In 1922, Einstein also traveled to Beijing where he gave four lectures at the most prominent university. Every Chinese scientist who could possibly attend, did so! Einstein spoke in English, which at the time few Chinese understood sufficiently, but a Chinese scientist of high standing translated his words with extraordinary skill.

Just before my parents returned home from the hospital, my father added:

"I tried to memorize Einstein's words when he returned to Shanghai after a trip to Japan and people complimented him on his achievements. They were published in an English language paper in Shanghai and I copied them into my little note-book of quotations, which I lost. But now, suddenly these words come back to my mind:

"'It is an irony of fate that I myself have been the recipient of excessive admiration and reverence from my fellow-beings, through no fault and no merit of my own.' "

Throughout the years, I spoke from time to time about Einstein with my father. His name kept coming up in the press, then on the radio, and eventually on television. I do believe what really attracted my idealistic father to Einstein was his pacifism and humanitarianism. Ever since Einstein's first visit to Shanghai in 1922, he became deeply concerned about injustice and suppression in China and often mentioned the subject. Social justice became a focus of his thoughts that propelled him to action. He fought racism and anti-Semitism, also taking strong stances against all war. In 1925, Einstein, together with Gandhi (1869–1948), and other important pacifists, signed a manifesto against compulsory military service. He had planned to visit Germany in March 1933, but due to the rise of the Nazis, Einstein proclaimed he would never set foot in German again—and he kept his word. He also cut all contacts to German institutions with which he had worked.

In 1933, Einstein immigrated to the United States. In 1940, he became a U.S. citizen (but also kept his original Swiss citizenship) and adopted Princeton as his new home.

The onset of World War II played an immense role in Einstein's life. Worries about atomic weapons, based on his scientific work, haunted him. As a result, he wrote a letter to U.S. President, Franklin Roosevelt, warning him of the danger of an atomic bomb. In 1943, the U.S. Navy employed Einstein's services as adviser for "highly explosive materials."

When the atomic bomb was dropped on Hiroshima on August 6, 1945, and three days later on Nagasaki on August 9, Einstein was deeply shocked. After the end of World War II, at a Nobel Memorial Dinner on December 10, he declared in a speech:

"The war is won, but peace is not."

A year later, in 1946, Einstein wrote an open letter to the United Nations, promoting the formation of a world government. He became the head of the Emergency Committee of Atomic Scientists whose aim remains till today the control of armament and the promotion of the peaceful use of nuclear energy.

After a long illness, Albert Einstein died peacefully in his bed on April 18, 1955, in Princeton, New Jersey.

After the war, we learned that three Chinese students, who had become American citizens, also won the Nobel Prize. In 1957, Tsung Dao Lee (Li Zhengdao) and Chen Ning Yang (Yang Zhenning) were jointly awarded the honor and, 19 years later in 1976, Samuel Chao Chung Ting (Ding Zhaozhong) was also bestowed the Nobel Prize. How proud the Chinese were of their sons!

Chapter 17

THE SHANGHAI VOLUNTEER CORPS AND BOY SCOUTS

Shanghailanders were justly proud of their Volunteer Corps (S.V.C.), which helped quell serious unrest in their city through many decades. On April 12, 1853, representatives of the International Settlement, Great Britain and the United States, held prolonged meetings resulting in the creation of the S.V.C. as a precautionary measure. The French Concession had a separate volunteer corps under the control of the French Consul General.

In 1932, when the Japanese landed their troops in Shanghai, the S.V.C. had 1,525 men, and the number of its volunteers reached 2,300 at the peak of the crisis. The S.V.C. guarded all entry points to the Settlements and held back the Japanese encroachers until the professional reinforcements arrived.

As the S.V.C.'s reputation grew, more and more volunteers joined, and it became an international defense force in Shanghai, subsidized by the Municipal Council of the International Settlement. By 1938, the S.V.C. incorporated various companies, among whom the American, the British, the Chinese, the Filipino, the Japanese, the Jewish, the Portuguese, the Scottish and the Russian. With the exception of the Russian Detachment of the S.V.C., all companies of the S.V.C., all civilian volunteers who manned the other companies were not remunerated for their efforts.

The Russian unit consisted of professionals. According to British journalist, Ralph Shaw, "they were superbly disciplined and impeccably turned out in British uniforms." They were paid salaries, which they richly deserved.

The first and only commander of the S.V.C. Jewish Company was Noel Jacobs, a Methodist British subject. He converted to Judaism after marrying his wife, a Russian Jewess, Dora Bogomolsky whose mother was a close, and much loved friend of my grandmother. My whole family deeply respected the Jacobs family, as did the entire Jewish Community and, one could say, all Shanghai.

Noel Jacobs was tall, pleasant looking, quiet, efficient, disciplined and very kind. He had an air of gentle authority, as well as a clear expectation that people act decently and do their best. Noel saw to it that the Jewish volunteers were professionally competent, were strictly drilled, learned to use various weapons and practiced setting up sandbags and barbed wire in case of attempted advances by the Japanese. In addition, due to local unrest, demonstrations and riots, Noel Jacobs insisted that the volunteers devote serious time to mob control.

The motto of the Jewish Company was:

"No advance without security."

The uniform of the Jewish Company was identical to that of the British

Boy Scouts in Shanghai, 1929.

Army before World War II, but the S.V.C. badge they wore on their collar had a superimposed Star of David.

In 1937, as the Japanese continued their attacks on Shanghai, the Jewish Company was sent to designated stations. 85 members were awarded the Municipal Council's Emergency Medal for their dedicated work. As Jewish refugees fleeing Nazi Europe started arriving in Shanghai, Noel Jacobs and his fellow volunteers helped them to settle in Shanghai.

After Pearl Harbor, in February 1942, the S.V.C. was disbanded by order of the Japanese who then occupied Shanghai. In September of that same year, a special order was published by the Corps headquarters notifying its units that "the Council has decided that there is no further necessity for the retention of the Shanghai Volunteer Corps and has approved its immediate disbandment." All further training and activity were suspended, and all weapons turned in. After 89 years, the S.V.C. disappeared from Shanghai.

One should add that, in addition to his dedication to the S.V.C., Noel Jacobs also had devoted much of his time, since 1923, to the Jewish 5th Shanghai Boy Scout Troop as Scoutmaster.

Shanghai was the first Chinese town to establish the "Scouts War Service," as Japanese attacks on the city increased. The Scouts' job was to help both civilians and the military to the best of their ability. Thirteen Chinese scouts, as well as one young girl carrying the Chinese flag were killed by Japanese fire. Inspired by their heroism, many youngsters of various nationalities rushed to join the organization and their number—including Girl Guides—finally reached over 15,000. The Shanghai scouts and girl guides had become international.

All scouts took a special oath:

The Scout Oath

On my honor I will do my best
To do my duty to God and my country
and to obey the Scout Laws
To help other people at all times
To keep myself physically strong
Mentally awake and morally straight

Noel Jacobs was an outstanding scoutmaster. During the postal strike on May 25, 1932, according to the *China Press*:

"*...The Council's temporary Post Office on the second floor of the Administration Building yesterday had a busy day...They were assisted by a number of the 5th Boy Scouts (Jewish Troop)... The Boy Scouts proved highly useful in directing callers, stamping coupons, sorting mail and other work...*"

On June 7, *The North-China Herald* reported:

"*...Boy Scouts, arranged through Scoutmaster Jacobs, did valuable work as messengers...*
... Boy Scouts yesterday were lending valuable aid in maintaining the air mail service..."

After "Pearl Harbor," Noel Jacobs was interned by the Japanese and remained imprisoned till the end of the war. Fortunately, his wife and three daughters had been evacuated earlier to the United States, as were many other families whom the Japanese considered "enemy nationals."

In 1949, Jacobs left Shanghai and returned to England to work for the British-American Tobacco Company who had originally employed him in Shanghai. He died in England in 1977 at the age of 79 and his wife passed away a few years later.

Until today, former Jewish Old China Hands have never forgotten Noel Jacobs and still revere him. On May 18, 1980, a forest of 3,500 trees was planted in Israel to commemorate his name.

Chapter 18

DECEMBER 8, 1941

On December 8, 1941, planes roared over Shanghai. It was early in the morning, before 7 a.m., Shanghai's citizens did not know as yet about the disaster of Pearl Harbor, nor did they imagine that Japanese planes would openly attack their city. Actually, people near the Bund had already heard heavy firing on the river even earlier, at 4 a.m. Yes, the Japanese no longer hid their aspirations to conquer one of the world's greatest cities, no longer apologized, no longer pretended an unintended error had occurred. They sank the British vessel *Petrel* and captured the U.S. vessel *Wake*. Both were small foreign gunboats patrolling the Whangpoo River.

The Captain of the *Petrel* valiantly refused to surrender, and dynamited their vessel which burst into fire. The crew, forced to jump into the Whangpoo, were picked up by sampans, then arrested by fully armed Japanese. The *Wake's* response was not so dramatic. Several days previously, the crew of the *Wake* had been transferred to the Philippines, as had all other American river patrol boats. A crew of only 25 sailors remained on board and surrendered to the Japanese *Bluejackets* (marines). By 10 a.m. that day, all Shanghai was occupied by Japanese troops.

The Japanese acted rapidly. It was obvious they had carefully prepared in advance the takeover of Shanghai. They closed newspapers, seized British properties, shut down the *North China Daily News* (a British newspaper) and the British bus company, but allowed public utilities to continue running, which included the Shanghai Power Company, the Shanghai Telephone

Company and the Shanghai Water Works. It was obvious they wanted the city to continue functioning. The entire International Settlement was in Japanese hands. The French Concession remained free, but later the Vichy Government gave in to Japanese pressure and handed over their territory to the puppet Nanking regime.

Shanghai began to change rapidly. Japanese khaki colored cars and camouflaged trucks raced through the streets as all other traffic moved in angry submission to the side. Most foreign cars had been requisitioned by the occupying forces. Besides, gasoline became very scarce, and was now mostly used for Japanese military vehicles. Double-decker busses disappeared and only single deck busses remained running on smoky charcoal. The French called them *gazogenes*. They were fitted with a weird contraption, somewhat similar to a stove, with a pipe belching dark smoke. Shanghai's traffic returned to the past: clumsy wheelbarrows, rickshaws, carts drawn by emaciated horses and the few remaining cars. Bicycles became the main

Japanese soldiers in Shanghai city during the war-time, under the advertisement of Coca Cola.

Refugees in the war.

method of transportation for most individuals. After Pearl Harbor, the number of bicycle licenses issued in the International Settlement and the French Concession quickly rose by 16,000.

In my diary I wrote:

"...One grape costs 30 cents, one egg 40 cents, a pair of shoes $800-$900 and a short rickshaw ride $15. A new currency called CRB (Central Reserve Bank) has replaced the old Fa Pi.

"We now live in the 'Great Asia Co-Prosperity Area' and are urged to 'chop up Anglo-Saxon Devils,' to 'butcher the U.S. and Britain'..."

Newspapers were ordered to publish almost daily notices such as:

"GENDARMERIE IN WESTERN SECTOR FORBIDS RUMORS

The Japanese General in the Western Area has issued a proclamation for the suppression of rumors to preserve peace and order in that Area.
OFFENDERS WILL BE SEVERELY PUNISHED"

The Japanese now considered Great Britain, the U.S., Holland and Belgium as their Number One Enemies and posted sentries at the entrance of their Consulates. In time, the Japanese Enemy Aliens Office in Hamilton House issued an order that all Number One Enemies should wear distinctive bright red armbands. The bands were 4 inches wide, and stamped with A for American, B for British, N for Netherlands (which included the Dutch and the Belgians), as well as with an individual registration number. The wearing of these bands was compulsory outside the home. People with red armbands were restricted from certain stores and public places. Eventually all were interned in Japanese concentration camps.

One day, Bob, my American boyfriend, told me that he and many other Enemy Nationals had been ordered to assemble outside the Community Church to await transfer to an unknown destination. There was no doubt whatsoever that this was bad news. When I arrived near the Community Church, I saw a rather large group that appeared mainly to consist of stateless Russians. Chinese were standing some distance away, probably for a last glance at their friends. Bob was tall, so I immediately distinguished him among the other unsmiling prisoners who each carried a suitcase. Some had bedding swung over their shoulders. Bob quickly caught sight of me and attempted a weak smile as well as a hardly noticeable hand sign. There were loud grunted commands from khaki-clad Japanese soldiers who motioned the prisoners to move rapidly towards Japanese military trucks and soon they were gone. The group who had come to see them off rapidly disbanded in all directions in order to get away as rapidly as possible from the Japanese soldiers.

Months later, there was a knock at the door. A rather frightened Chinese man stood there. Amah called me to speak to him. He had brought me a message from Bob who was in the Pootung (Pudong) camp. His words appeared to have been hurriedly written. He mentioned that he had access to a secret radio in camp. He and his friends listened to a "musical request" program from which they got information. He asked me to request "for Bob" the song *Stormy Weather* if I intended to give him up and *Danny Boy* if I intended to wait for him till after the War. From then on, to comfort him, I daily requested that *Danny Boy* be played, although our romance had not been a serious one, just a matter of going out dancing occasionally, discussing the state of the world, and taking long walks. Still, my heart ached for him and I hoped to provide, at least, a little bit of comfort.

When I showed my parents the letter, or rather scribbled note from Bob, they panicked. They worried about the consequences both for him and for me. With youthful optimism, I was convinced everything would be alright and, very fortunately, nothing tragic resulted. Bob was later repatriated to the U.S. in a prisoners' exchange. I saw him just once for a very short time before his departure. He seemed to be changed, even thinner than before, and looked grim. Since then, I often wondered what had become of him. Once I was told by a Russian friend, who had left on a convoluted trip to the U.S. with other refugees, that when the ship landed for a stopover in South Africa, a man named Bob had come on board, looking for me and asking people if they knew me. Some did, but they did not have my address handy. We never met again.

In Shanghai, the Bridge House was notorious as a place of torture and death. John Powell, editor of the *China Weekly Review*, was imprisoned there by the Japanese. He had always been very forthright in his writings, very concerned about injustice towards the Chinese, and fearless. Being a much-respected man in Shanghai, he became one of the early victims of the Japanese. He suffered indescribable torture before he was finally released in a prisoner exchange. He reached the U.S. but died shortly after from the aftermath of his ordeal in Bridge House. His weight had gone down from 140 lbs. to 70 lbs., and he could no longer stand due to the weakness and the deteriorated condition of his feet.

In the meantime, I copied in my diary an article in an English language Chinese paper about a prisoner of war camp in Taiwan. Obviously, I did not believe a word of it.

FORMER ALLIED COMMANDERS LEAD NORMAL PEACEFUL LIFE IN TAIWAN CAMP.

(A Taiwan War Prisoners' Camp. February 15, Domei)

While most of them (Americans), after their dismal defeats suffered, freely admitted that the treatment received has been magnanimous, particularly General Wainright, who said he owed a debt of gratitude in a personal letter to the Japanese authorities...The bill of fare consists chiefly of vegetables but meat is added periodically, despite the fact that the Japanese themselves are denying this item of food as much as possible. Since the prisoners measure beyond the standard of the average Japanese, ample sized beds with soft mattresses are provided especially for the sake of comfort...The War prisoners are allowed to buy cigarettes freely, which is a wartime luxury for anybody, while phonograph concerts are held three times a week to lighten the spirit which is prone to turn gloomy despite the relatively favorable conditions of detention. The easy, yet systematic routine, has enabled the men to gain enormously in weight, compared to the famished and weary condition in which they were brought from the fronts...

U.S. Forces rescued General Wainwright from the Japanese in August 1945, in time to participate in the Surrender Ceremony aboard the U.S.S. Missouri. He was emaciated after years of starvation and later people disclosed he had been severely beaten by Japanese guards on many occasions.

Chapter 19

CITY OF REFUGE

One evening Shura (Russian abbreviation for Alexander) Olmert dropped in for a discussion with my father. Olmert was the uncle of the present Prime Minister of Israel, Ehud Olmert. He, like my father, was an idealistic man and they often had long conversations. That evening their discussion concentrated on the growing influence of Nazis in Shanghai. A couple of years before a group of Nazis had occupied a top story suite in the Park Hotel, a 16-story building across the street from the Race Course. At the time, the Park was considered to be a huge skyscraper, but today many higher buildings dwarf it.

My father, as he sipped his strong tea, said in a worried tone: "The Nazis are pouring more and more openly into Shanghai. It is no longer an infiltration but a powerful river! This became quite obvious some time ago. During the autumn races they threw out of their hotel window hundreds of anti-Semitic leaflets written in English and Chinese, in the direction of the Race Course. I shall never forget that!"

Shura put down his glass of steaming tea and replied heatedly:

"Neither will I! Never! It was the first public anti-Jewish demonstration that had ever taken place in Shanghai. I don't know if the Nazis had studied the direction of the wind, but the fact is that the wind blew the propaganda leaflets right into huge crowds of Chinese and foreigners watching the horses dash by."

"Yes," my father responded, "A well-calculated plan or plain good luck for those criminals!"

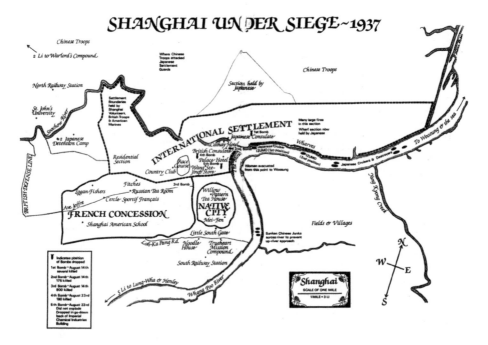

Map of Shanghai under siege, 1937.

Both men were very excited since on that day an article had appeared in one of the local English papers, which the Japanese had copied from a Nazi propaganda booklet, *Two Men in a Boat*, the two men being Roosevelt and Churchill. It claimed that President Roosevelt was a "paid servant of the Jews" and surrounded by a group of rapacious financiers and money sharks, resentful and vindictive Jews and other rogues. Roosevelt sought re-election to a third term by deliberate lying...

By the summer of 1939, it was obvious that Hitler was planning to exterminate all Jews in Germany and other countries where he had gained control. Shanghai was the only place in the world where Jewish refugees could land without a visa, nor proof of capital. By the end of June, 14,500 German, Austrian and Czechoslovakian Jews had arrived in Shanghai and, before the year ended, 5,000 more desperate refugees landed. At the time, the northern section of the city, Hongkew, had been taken over by the Japanese and they were steadily encroaching on the rest of the city. Many foreigners in Shanghai had already been repatriated, firms had moved to Manila, Hong Kong or Singapore.

The tragic fact was that no other city anywhere had offered the fleeing refugees shelter. Since rents in Hongkew were cheaper than elsewhere in Shanghai, most refugees moved into the area. Some managed to find jobs in the International Settlement and the French Concession. Although various committees had been organized by Shanghai Jews to help the penniless newcomers, many were depressed and suffered from ill health. Until Pearl Harbor, American Jews provided important financial help to the refugees but after December 8, 1941, this direct contact became impossible.

The refugees found it very difficult to adjust to local conditions. They were not used to boiling water, washing vegetables and fruit in hot water or potassium permanganate, and suffered from frequent stomach trouble, attacks of worms, and dysentery. Besides, most reacted strongly to shots against cholera, typhoid and smallpox, to which Shanghailanders and Shanghainese had become used since early childhood. For unaccustomed refugees these injections often resulted in red swollen arms and fever. Some were incapacitated for days. In addition, Shura and my father discussed the great difficulty for the refugees to find work. Many could not speak English, and though sometimes willing, could not replace work done by coolies. This was unheard of in Shanghai. Besides, they would have been unable to survive on the money paid for such labor.

On February 18, 1943, a proclamation was issued by the "Commander-in-Chief of the Imperial Japanese Army in the Shanghai Area" and the "Commander-in-Chief of the Imperial Japanese Navy in the Shanghai Area" that restricted the places of residence and business of European refugees who had arrived in Shanghai after 1937, to a "Designated Area" in Hongkew. The next day, an item appeared in the local papers stating that a Jewish refugee had committed suicide by taking nitric acid. The last sentence of the notice was what inspired fury in my father and Shura Olmert: "The reasons for this decision are unknown."

Jewish committees to help the refugees worked feverishly to help them settle in *HEIME* (collective homes), receive at least minimal quantities of food, medical care, and open schools for children. Deep gloom descended upon the newcomers. The one favorable aspect was that the Chinese surrounding

Refuge Pao Chia in Hongkew, 1944.

them, many of whom lived in worse conditions of poverty, always treated them in a kindly manner and many refugees had very friendly contacts with them. As my father often said:

"We must never forget how Shanghai opened its doors to miserable Jewish refugees and how decently the Chinese, in general, treated them."

The story of Polish Jewish refugees in Shanghai was a different one from those who had fled from Germany, Austria and Czechoslovakia. As German Nazi armies advanced, some 2,000 Poles had fled from Poland, including a group of 300 members (faculty and students) of Mir Yeshiva (a religious academy) who had crossed the Russian border and escaped to neighboring Lithuania.

In Lithuania, a humane Japanese Consul General in Kaunus (Kovno), Sempo (Chiune) Sugihara, granted the Jewish refugees transit visas through

Japan to Curacao against the instructions of the Japanese government. In despair, the Polish refugees streamed to Consul Sugihara, who issued transit visas valid only for ten days. If necessary, he extended them again and again. Sugihara's wife Yukiko, assisted him day and night, stamping the "visas for life" —as historians later called them. These false visas permitted the Poles to leave Lithuania. The visas to Curacao were also illegally stamped by the kind-hearted Dutch Consul in Kaunus, since potential immigrants were obliged to first obtain landing permits from the Governor of Curacao. These landing permits were unavailable to the Poles.

When the Jewish refugees arrived in Kobe, they were not stopped from entering Japan. The Kobe Jewish community extended all the necessary help to them, but as Pearl Harbor approached, Japanese suspicions of foreigners reached new heights. The close ties of the Mir Yeshiva with friends and supporters in America became regarded as dangerous. In Japan, they were now considered as potential agents for the U.S. Finally, the Japanese government announced its decision to ship the Jewish refugees away from Japan to China, to the city of now Japanese controlled Shanghai. Of course, this news hit the Mir Yeshiva like a lightning bolt: once again they were to be uprooted and sent to a strange destination.

My grandfather's friend, Shanghai's Rabbi, Meir Ashkenazi, conducted negotiations with Silas Hardoon and succeeded in receiving his permission for the Mir Yeshiva to occupy the Beit Aharon Synagogue, which Hardoon had built. The Mir Yeshiva remained in Shanghai until 1947.

One day, in 1944, I received a letter from my friend Heinz, who had been forced to move to the Restricted Area in Hongkew, to which today many refer to as the Shanghai Ghetto. Heinz was a pleasant, courteous, nice-looking boy, the only member of his family to escape from Berlin. He was only 15 years old at the time. I met him when my mother brought him home to dinner. All our family was very fond of him. Heinz begged me to come and visit him since Ghoya, who handled the issue of permits for refugees to leave the Restricted Area, had yelled at him and refused to give him the required paper. Outsiders could freely enter the Restricted Area, so Heinz who really longed to see me begged me to visit him.

My parents refused to allow me to go alone over the Garden Bridge to Hongkew and, finally, my mother agreed to accompany me. She too worried about Heinz. In fact, since it was cold, she took out an old coat she had once bought simply to give away in case of need. The coat had a fur lining. She was certain that Heinz must have been freezing because of the reduced intake of food he was given and probably had no heating where he lived.

On the Garden Bridge, our tram stopped in front of Japanese sentries. Everyone was compelled to bow to these representatives of the Emperor of Japan, then the soldiers grasping a bayonet in one hand, signaled the tram to continue on its journey with a wave of their free arm.

My father had managed to acquire for Heinz a Certificate of Employment required by the Japanese before giving a permit to leave the Restricted Area. But one day Heinz stood in line for hours and when he finally appeared before Ghoya, the Japanese was in a furious mood and refused to grant it.

"I will not try again," Heinz told us. "I cannot go through this once more!"

When we approached the Restricted Area, we saw that it was surrounded by barbed wire with several control points for entry and exit. At the gates stood several uniformed Japanese, as well as refugee members of the Pao Chia, an auxiliary police who were expected to check passes, keep order and enforce curfew regulations. Of course, the refugee Pao Chia was under the control and power of the Japanese forces.

Heinz stood some 20 yards away from the gate. He greeted us with great joy and my mother hugged him. She examined his face, found he had got thinner and the first question she asked was:

"Are you getting enough to eat?"

"Well," Heinz replied, "the Kitchen Fund Committee sees to it that we get a minimum of 3,150 calories a day, and children get an extra meal in the evening."

Heinz pointed out to us some 40 blocks of dilapidated looking buildings which were the *Heime* (homes), lanes where refuse and rubble gathered and street vendors sold boiled drinking water, but refused to show us his room, which must have been really miserable.

I asked him about reading material and he said they had three German language dailies, one of which was named in English, *Shanghai Jewish Chronicle*, but was actually published in German.

"Really," he said, "our intellectual life is quite active. We have classical musicians, actors, a school for adults, and school for carpenters, engineers, electricians, and mechanics. Lectures are organized. There is a good school for children. Yes, I cannot say that we are mentally starved, but we do have health problems. People really do not eat a healthy diet and many catch all kinds of diseases which we never even knew existed when we lived in Germany."

I had never been in Europe but in spite of all the squalor, the Restricted Area somehow reflected a tinge of Europe. A sign advertised a *Viennese Tailor for the Man of Taste,* and a haberdashery, the *Royal Glover* displayed signs in German, English, Chinese and Japanese. My mother asked Heinz if there was a place where we could have tea and he led us up a narrow winding staircase, to a small space on the roof with a few tables and folding chairs. An elderly violinist played Austrian walzes, and we were served a surprisingly tasty *Kuchen* (cake).

Heinz was very grateful for the warm coat my mother had brought. We sat "catching up" on many subjects and finally left with a heavy heart, not knowing when we would see him. Tragically, we did not meet again. Right after the war ended, Heinz found out that all his family had been exterminated in Germany and committed suicide.

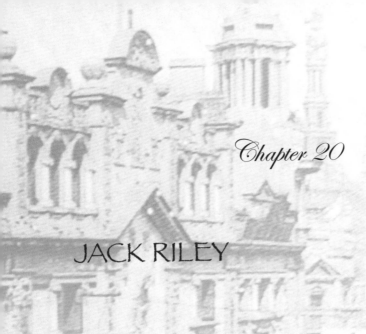

Chapter 20

JACK RILEY

One day, when I arrived for my class on Abnormal Psychology at the Aurora University, the young Jesuit Brother teaching us the course announced that he had made arrangements for us to visit a psychiatric ward. The doctors explaining their cases would present a number of patients to us. As we all got ready to leave, I had a strong feeling of foreboding increased by the appearance of the building we entered. It was a block of red brick, with a dark interior and clearly locked doors. As we walked through, we heard strange animal-like cries.

Our group of students was gathered in a large room facing several doctors. Chairs were lined up prepared for students to sit on. The first woman patient, led by two tough and unsmiling nurses, cackled with laughter, talked to herself and stared at our young Jesuit. Suddenly, she sprinted towards him with lighting speed. The alert nurses managed to grab her and held her back as she proclaimed her love for him, accompanied by terrifying laughter. We all sat frozen in our seats as a psychiatrist explained her case, apparently connected with nymphomania. My reaction was great pity for the patient, obviously imprisoned for her own safety and that of others. It was indeed a painful experience.

As the second patient was brought in, I cowered in my chair, trying to hide behind the back of a student in front of me. I knew this patient! A couple of years previously, when searching for my own Jewish identity, I told my parents I would like to study Hebrew. My mother soon found a young Polish refugee from the Mir Yeshiva. During our private class at home, he always

UNIVERSITÉ L'AURORE
SHANG-HAI

學　大　旦　震　海　上

CERTIFICAT D'EXAMEN

L'UNIVERSITÉ L'AURORE certifie que

Mlle _Rabinovich_

d e _Shanghai_ a obtenu à l'examen

de _Première_ année de Faculté de Médecine

Section la note _76.1_

et qu'il est apte à entrer en _seconde_ année.

Shang-hai, le _30 Juin 1943_

Le Chancelier :

中華民國

月

日給

教務長

學生

於醫學院

考試得 76.1 分准予升入第 年

肄業此證

系第 年

縣人

升級證書

Author's Certificate from Faculty of Medicine, Aurora University, 1943.

sat at a distance from me and never looked at me in the face. Our lessons continued for a few weeks, then he stopped coming and I did not pursue the matter. Later, I heard that he had had an appendicitis attack and, was taken to a hospital where he mistrusted all those surrounding him. When a doctor approached him to prepare him for the operation, he stabbed him to death with a knife he had concealed. And now, here he was, insane!

"Are there any Jews here?" he cried in Yiddish, Polish and Russian. "Save me!"

My blood froze. After the war ended, I heard he had been transferred to an American hospital in the United States. I am not sure of the veracity of this rumor.

The last couple of patients were twins, two teen-age girls. They snarled and, lashed out at their attendants, trying to bite, hit and scratch them. One could really compare them to two wild animals. The professor proceeded calmly with his explanations and when the girls were finally dragged out of the room, he said:

"The patients you saw are the twin daughters of Jack Riley."

Jack Riley! A famous mobster whose name most probably everyone in Shanghai had heard. Nobody had ever mentioned his insane twins. In fact, until this very day, I have never read anywhere about their existence. Had I not studied medicine, and had we not been taken to the psychiatric ward, I would never have suspected this secret in Riley's life. When I asked a Chinese doctor's assistant who their mother was, he said he did not know but as long as Riley remained in Shanghai, a generous monthly check would arrive regularly for his daughters' upkeep.

Riley, a mobster and fugitive from justice in the U.S., had entered Shanghai without any problem. Our city was an open Treaty Port and visitors were controlled only superficially. Riley spent 15 very profitable years in Shanghai, operated slot machines (and he was named "Shanghai's Slot Machines King"), bars—also in the infamous "Blood Alley"—as well as night-clubs and restaurants. Blood Alley was under the control of the French police, some of whom had obviously been bribed and closed their eyes to the goings-on there. Nevertheless, Black Maria, the French police van, frequently was compelled to enter the area in order to break up violent fights. Policemen would forcefully handcuff troublemakers and take them to the police station.

The popular Shanghai radio broadcaster, Carroll Alcott, wrote in his book *My War with Japan (1943)* that Riley had been fingerprinted in the U.S. before his escape from prison and although he had disfigured his fingertips with acid and some self-executed surgery, he had failed to remove all the telling lines.

His prints were sent to Washington, where the Federal Bureau of Investigation did a remarkable job of reconstruction. Riley's records were traced, even to the doctor who officiated at his birth. This was revealed in the United States Court of China on the first day of his trial… Riley was returned to the United States to serve 18 months in the federal prison at McNeil Island and to face his uncompleted sentence in Oklahoma…

In 1940, when the Japanese virtually occupied all Shanghai, Jack Riley was arrested for operating a gambling den, but he escaped, helped by the Japanese to whom he paid large sums of "protection money." It was reputed that Riley also had close connections with Big Ears Du Yue-Sheng, the powerful gangster.

That evening at dinner, after our University's visit to the psychiatric ward, I told my parents about my horrible experience, seeing my former Hebrew teacher interned, and the two terrifying daughters of Jack Riley.

My father replied, that through his Company, he had had some dealings with the mobster, supplying his restaurants with Sperry flour.

"Of course," my father added. "our business with him was strictly legal, but Riley did make me feel very uncomfortable. He had a charming way about him, but exuded an atmosphere of danger, like a poisonous snake!"

As to my Hebrew teacher, my father knew he had ended up in a psychiatric ward but had no further information about him.

Chapter 21

U.S. BOMBING

U.S. air- raids over Shanghai were intensifying. B-29s zoomed over the city leaving long white trails that slowly dissipated. The Japanese called the attackers *B-niju-ku*, a literal translation of B-29. Local newspapers published frequent instructions regarding action to be taken during such bombings, headlining them: *Notice of Immediate Importance.* One such notice stated:

l. Sirens
Precautionary period: one 2-minute blast
Air-raid: seven 5-second blasts
All clear: two 15-second blasts

2. Flags and lamps
Precautionary period: 2 green flags or 2 green lamps
Air-raid: 2 red flags or 2 red lamps
All clear: 2 yellow flags or 2 yellow lamps

As the sirens sounded, everyone stopped and started counting them. After an air-raid, all newspapers published announcements similar to these:

"Sirens sound here as U.S. planes scout around and scurry off, having sustained severe damage in frontal attacks with the Japanese Air Force."

Or

"Enemy machines beat a hasty retreat upon being detected by Japanese planes."

U.S. planes.

The truth is that B-29's flew at a height of 50,000 ft. at tremendous speed. The Japanese started building the *Raiden* (Thunderbolt) plane to try to hit them but production was very slow, so that B-29 attacks were very short and very deadly.

Whenever an attack occurred while we were at the Aurora University, all students rushed cheering to the windows in spite of the efforts of the Jesuit Fathers to calm us. If repetitive raids continued, classes were dismissed.

On July 17, 1945, B-29's bombed the Restricted Area in Hongkew where the Japanese had concealed a naval station that directed Japanese warships in the Pacific. It was a hot, sticky day. The sky was cloudy. Seven siren blasts warned against the air-raid but, by then, bombs had already started to fall and detonate. A friend later told me that he was riding a bicycle and rushing home when an armed Japanese stopped him, grabbed the bicycle and speeded away. Buildings were destroyed, some people were killed and many were wounded.

Most houses in Hongkew had no cellars, thus in order to protect themselves from flying shards, families would pile mattresses on tables and huddle under them on the floor for protection during air-raids.

As soon as the raid had begun, my father had received an urgent call from a member of one of his committees and immediately took off on his bicycle.

He returned home hours later, grey and exhausted, and told us of numerous communications from Jewish refugees who were overwhelmed by the devoted and courageous cooperation of the Chinese. Refugee doctors, nurses and civilians immediately organized themselves and took action. Chinese living in the same district rushed to their aid, carrying the dead and the wounded, tearing cloth into bandages and bringing water. Jewish refugees and Chinese worked side by side like brothers. On that day, 31 refugees died, and hundreds were wounded. Hundreds of Chinese were also killed and wounded.

The day following the bombing, it started raining and water poured into buildings through ruined roofs and walls, damaging the interior of rooms and the few belongings the refugees and Chinese had managed to accumulate. Humidity, dust and fragments left hundreds of people completely poverty stricken.

That night, a friend called me from Hongkew. He told me not to worry, that the reaction on the part of the refugees and the Chinese had been remarkable.

"All the wounded, whether refugees or Chinese, were cared for without any discrimination whatsoever," he asserted in an excited voice. "Dispensaries were set up with lightning speed. Even beggars were treated like everyone else."

When I repeated these words to my father, he exclaimed:

"Zamechatelno! Zamechatelno! (In Russian: 'Wonderful! Wonderful!') Hitler has not been able to destroy the Jewish spirit and centuries of repression have not killed the inherent goodness of the Chinese people!"

My mother immediately started collecting cans of food from our small emergency stock and added toys for children from her store to take to Hongkew at the earliest possibility.

That night, a very good friend of mine, Sidney, an "Overseas Chinese" from Indonesia visited my family to share news he had heard on an illegal short-wave radio he secretly possessed: thousands of leaflets had been dropped by the Americans over 11 Japanese cities. Unless the Japanese surrendered, fierce air attacks would continue. In a post-war book published by Isoko Hatano, the author wrote:

"... Women hereabouts are terrified of the leaflets...According to most people, they were not dropped for benevolent reasons. However, magnanimous a man is, he is considered a traitor if he acts against the strategic needs of his country..."

Nobody in Shanghai really knew how matters stood. Power shortages increased:

NEW LIGHT REGULATIONS

ALL SHOPS AND BUSINESSES SHOULD BE CLOSED BY 7.00 P.M... SHOULD THEY VIOLATE THE REGULATIONS, BUSIENSSES WILL RECEIVE A WARNING; A SECOND OFFENSE IS TO RESULT IN THE CUTTING OF POWER SUPPLY AND A FINE; A THIRD WILL BE PUNISHED BY A 10-DAY BUSINESS SUSPENSION AND A FOURTH BY WITHDRAWAL OF BUSINESS LICENSE.

Our family, friends, neighbors and everyone in Shanghai prepared themselves for an unknown, menacing future. As to me, I refused to change my schedule, rode my bike daily to the University, halted when a barricade was erected by the Japanese, then dashed onwards. I continued to assiduously prepare for examinations, often sitting under the staircase for safety, should a sudden air raid occur. During that first year of Medicine, we were expected to memorize a great deal and were sometimes given as much as four hours to complete our papers under the watchful eyes of Jesuit who wanted to be sure that nobody cheated. Not only did we have to write what we had learned, but also draw by heart diagrams and graphics. Should the sirens suddenly go off when I was deep in study under the staircase, the rest of the family would hurriedly join me. Once, as I concentrated on a forthcoming Osteology examination, my mother sitting next to me asked in a puzzled voice:

"How can you possibly concentrate? The whole house is shaking!"

I glanced up, heard glass tinkle, saw the curtains sway in front of the windows in the hall, and went right back to studying whatever bones we had been assigned. At this moment, my only concern was to pass the test.

Chapter 22

PACIFIC WAR UNWINDING

On July 23, 1945, my father and heads of 18 Jewish organizations in Shanghai wrote a letter to the Japanese authorities addressed to:

> Mr. T. Kubota,
> Director General,
> The Office of the Stateless Refugees Affairs,
> Present.

I have a copy of this letter till today. After the letter was sent, our family, and probably those of all the signatories worried. How would the Japanese react to this daring proposal? Would there be arrests? Would the people whose names appeared be sent to the infamous Bridge House?

Here is the content of the letter:

Sir,

We, the undersigned representatives of all organizations of the local Ashkenazi Jewish Community, deeply moved by the events of the 17ᵗʰ instant, and greatly concerned with the fate of the refugees residing in the Designated Area, are taking herewith the liberty of approaching you with the following appeal:

The disaster of the 17ᵗʰ inst. which resulted in the death of 31 refugees, and wounding of nearly 300 refugees, and which caused irreparable loss to many hundred refugee families whose lodgings were demolished, has brought about amongst them a feeling of utter despondency.

The fact that of all the European population only refugees were affected by the

Aus Melchiors "Ghoya-Mappe"

REFUGEE AND GHOYA 1944
& (REFUGEE ARTIST)

Refugee and Ghoya,
1944.

disaster causes them to feel that their stay in the Designated Area singles them out for the most horrible fate. Although losses are unavoidable during the war, no such feelings would have arisen had they been given freedom to move and to reside elsewhere, and a similar disaster would have had a different psychological aspect. The apprehensions of the Jewish refugee population find some justification in the fact that the Designated Area stretches over a former war-torn district. Most of the houses there were hastily and carelessly rebuilt during the recent years and cannot withstand any shock.

According to the opinion of doctors attending the wounded, most fatalities were due to the crumbling of houses and with many houses there being now shattered, it is beyond any doubt that further shocks will cause increased fatalities.

In view of the above, we believe that now it is most desirable to grant the refugee population in the Designated Area freedom to remove their living quarters to other parts of the city. We believe that granting of such right will cause no immediate mass exodus from the Area as living accommodation is now very scarce.

The granting of freedom to the refugees to move and to reside will nevertheless have a most salutary psychological effect and help to alleviate the painful feelings caused by the recent disaster. Such an act would be hailed by the refugees and by all the Jews as a most kind, timely and humanitarian action of the Authorities.

We hope most sincerely that this appeal will be granted by you.

We remain
Most respectfully yours

This letter was followed by the names of the 18 organizations and signatures of their heads. My father's signed his name on the list beside the title of his publication *Our Life.*

That afternoon, Sidney arrived with his tennis racket to take me to the courts for a game. We played tennis together as often as we could manage. It was also an opportunity to rest between sets and spend some time together.

As soon as we started walking, I expressed to Sidney my deep worry about the consequences of the appeal. One never knew what the occupying army would decide to do. Tears stood in my eyes. Putting a consoling arm around my shoulders, Sidney said:

"Please don't worry so much! Your father will be safe. The Japanese have much more serious concerns now. Last night, when I listened to the British news, they announced that there is no longer any doubt whatsoever that the war is coming to an end. The Allies are giving the Japanese mortal blows. They are on the verge of collapsing."

I nodded and managed to enjoy our tennis game.

Time passed and still there was no reaction from the Japanese authorities to the letter of July 23. Sidney came over almost daily and reported developments he had heard, facts that made it clear that the Pacific War was unwinding. In Shanghai, people began to whisper:

"When will the Americans land? How many Shanghai citizens can survive street fighting here?"

It was common knowledge that no place was safe since the Japanese had

Japanese in Shanghai during the war-time, painted by Austrian artist Friedrich Schiff.

godowns (warehouses) and ammunition dumps in every section of our city.

The Japanese had ordered everyone to excavate a dug out in front of their homes and now pavements were pierced with thousands of holes. A futile attempt! It was certainly doubtful they would be useful in an air raid, but they did cause many accidents, especially after dark during black outs when people stumbled into them. Avenue Joffre was hardly recognizable. It had been transformed from an elegant boulevard into a row of neglected and almost empty shops, each with a big, deep hole dug in front of it. Prices rose to inconceivable heights as money devalued. According to my diary, meat cost $22,000 per lb. and one egg $1,000.

On August 1, a bomb exploded two blocks away from our home and I sat under the stairs writing *MY LAST WILL AND TESTAMENT* in case I were killed in bombing or for any other reason.

After rereading the above "Will," I found it was ridiculous and did not complete it. I thought of tearing it up, changed my mind, and kept it among all my other papers. Its aim was mainly to comfort my parents assuring them that I had had a very happy life and "better a short life and a full one than a long and empty one."

In the meantime, Sidney reported that according to British broadcasts, U.S. submarines, as well as mines dropped by Allied planes near Japan's coast, had cut off the flow of war materials to the Japanese. No more oil for refineries, no more bauxite for aluminum plants, no more iron ore for steel mills. Everyone including the old and the weak were hurriedly drafted but there were no weapons available for them. Shamelessly, the Japanese authorities blamed their countrymen for not having fought the enemy hard enough!

On August 9, 1945, a disturbing article was reprinted in the local English papers from the Tokyo *Mainichi:*

"ATTACHED TO PARACHUTES

A small number of enemy B-29s penetrated into Hiroshima on August 6 shortly before 8 a.m. and dropped a number of explosive bombs, as a result of which a considerable number of houses in the city were destroyed and fire broke out at various places.

It seems the enemy dropped new-type bombs attached to parachutes which exploded in the air. Although details are still under investigation, their explosive power cannot be made light of."

The Japanese called the new weapon *pikadon, pik* meaning "blinding light" and *don* referring to the dreadful sound it created.

On August 10, the Japanese press mentioned another *pikadon* being dropped over Nagasaki, claiming the damage had not been as "serious" as in Hiroshima.

Much later, we found out that soon after the second atomic bombing by the U.S., General Anami who had vowed to continue fighting till the last Japanese, committed *Harakiri* (ritual suicide). His body, in full-dress uniform, was placed in a small office room and soldiers filed past him crying bitterly. Later his body was carried in a casket to the top of a hill. After covering the casket with dried twigs, cans of gasoline were poured over it and set to fire by a colonel, who threw a lighted match towards the body of the general. Soldiers saluted while his grief stricken family watched the entire proceedings.

In Shanghai, things turned suddenly quiet. No more bombings. Wild rumors circulated: the war was over, the war would continue, Japan would never give up. Then unexpectedly, Shanghai citizens found out that Russia had denounced the Russo-Japanese Neutrality Pact and declared war on Japan. Great jubilation! Sidney rushed over saying he had heard on the British radio that "from August 9 the Soviet Union will consider herself in a state of war against Japan." On the same day, the Japanese offered to surrender if Emperor Hirohito would be retained.

Finally, I stopped worrying about my father. Yes, the Japanese did indeed have greater concerns now! Sidney was celebrating with us when our phone rang. Peace had been declared! All over Shanghai, the black out was over. Lights appeared in every window. People crowded the streets shouting with joy, drinking, laughing. Total strangers hugged each other. U.S. and Chinese flags suddenly appeared. Shanghailanders and Shanghainese, waved them fearlessly. Japanese troops disappeared from the streets.

After U.S. soldiers arrived in Shanghai, our friend Max Scheidlinger who had been restricted to the Designated Area and hated Ghoya for the humiliation and misery he had caused, phoned us. Among the first batch of

U.S. soldiers was one of his distant relatives who dropped in to visit him. Max had temporarily remained in Hongkew because lack of funds prevented him from moving back to the International Settlement. When Max described to his relative how sadistically Ghoya had treated the refugees who came to apply for permits, his relative responded angrily:

"Let's go find him and beat him up!"

They then proceeded to a camp where all the Japanese awaited transportation back to Japan and looked around until they found Ghoya. When he saw their furious faces, Ghoya fell on his knees and begged for mercy. He kept repeating:

"I never killed anyone! Never killed anyone!"

That was not to be his first beating. Other former refugees had already taken revenge on him, but his two visitors were not moved and showed him no mercy.

On August 16, Shanghai listened to an excellent English translation of Emperor Hirohito's Imperial Rescript. While millions of Japanese sobbed as they heard for the first time their Emperor Hirohito speaking directly and personally to them. The Japanese called it "The Voice of the Crane." In a lengthy speech, Hirohito officially announced Japan's surrender. He was not charged for war crimes but was forced to renounce his divine status, proclaiming his "non-divinity" on January 1, 1946. The Allies permitted him to retain the title of "Head of State."

Chapter 23

JAPANESE INTERNMENT CAMPS

My mother knew a number of people who had been interned in Shanghai Japanese camps. Right after the war ended, she could hardly wait to visit them and bring them whatever they could use. Some of the internees were her former British, American or Dutch *Peter Pan* shop customers.

After the middle of August 1945, my mother and I took off by bicycle to Lunghwa (Longhua) Camp. My short mother was riding her child-size bike, so the going was slow. The camp was situated about eight miles southwest of the Bund on Minghong Road (about 2 miles from the Lunghwa airport) and located in the former Kiangsu Shanghai Middle School. This school had been heavily damaged during the 1937 Sino-Japanese hostilities.

During our ride there, one of my bicycle tires burst, both to my mother's and my great annoyance. Since there was no tire repairman in sight, I had to continue the trip on foot while my mother rode by my side as slowly as she could. She had brought along, attached to the back of her bike, a big parcel of oatmeal, flour, oil and home-made cookies. The heat was oppressive and we arrived exhausted and bathed in perspiration.

From afar, the camp looked welcoming: a number of large buildings surmounted by Allied flags. But as we approached, we realized the old buildings were in disrepair and the grounds were overgrown with weeds. The camp, housing 1,988 internees, consisted of seven concrete buildings,

A ceremony in memory of Holocaust victims, 1945.

three wooden barracks (originally used by the Japanese as stabling) and several outbuildings. We later learned that 59 dorms and 127 rooms had been assigned to families. During the war a number of prisoners attempted escapes, nine of whom actually succeeded and reached free China.

We found my mother's friends after some searching. They had changed in a way that was hard to describe. It was not only that they had lost weight, but the dark suntan they acquired while washing clothes outside in canals and digging vegetable gardens did little to hide their haggard appearance. Moreover, their expressions had altered: the joy of life seemed to be gone, their faces reflected sad submission. Although we were very simply dressed, we appeared almost elegant in comparison to the detainees whose clothes were ragged.

Mrs. Eliot, a former customer of my mother's who used to order beautiful children's clothes in my mother's store, told us that once in winter when she was trying to do her laundry outside, she fainted from cold and hunger. All they had had that day was a bowl of *congee*, very watery rice. My mother and

I were embarrassed when Mrs. Eliot admired our "beautiful blouses" and "Oh! Such healthy looks!"

Mrs. Eliot was delighted with the gifts my mother brought and shared them with some of my mother's other acquaintances. She thanked us repeatedly. We wished we could have carried more for them.

We dared not ask too many questions, but Mrs. Eliot seemed glad to talk freely. She told us:

"We did make a great effort to try and improve our lives as much as possible, but the Japanese guards were so unpredictable and so unjust, that they managed to destroy the spirit of many internees. We tried hard to keep our chins up and struggle on, grew vegetables and kept our quarters as orderly as possible, all the while living out of suitcases with hardly any privacy. People took the initiative to organize classes for children and adults and even entertainment, some of which was really good by any standards, but the years took their toll, years of humiliation and often cruelty. It was really hard to keep our spirits up, much as we tried. All we long for now is to get out of the camp and be free. Freedom! What a wonderful word!"

That evening when my father returned from work, my mother and I told him about our trip to Lunghwa. He thought a while and said:

"I will go tomorrow to the Pootung Camp to look for my former British boss at Dodwell's. I really wonder how he is doing and want to take some food for him as well as reading material."

My sister and I both chimed in:

"Can we come with you?"

My father readily agreed and early next morning we took a launch across the Whangpoo River to the Pootung Internment Camp. We were shocked at its appearance. In comparison to Pootung Camp, Lungwha looked like a resort! Yes, an effort had been made when the war ended to decorate the water tower with a white painted cross and flags of the Allied nations, but the misery of the area could not be disguised.

The building where our father's former British boss now lived with some 1,000 other bachelors was once a *godown* (warehouse). It appeared that the men had made little effort to make it livable: everywhere disorder, a mess of unmade beds, cooking utensils and clothing. Father's boss, once a haughty gentleman, always impeccably dressed with beautiful ties, was toothless, shrunken and wore dirty shorts. He had been taken to Pootung with the first batch of internees in late January 1943.

The warehouse where they located him had once belonged to the British American Tobacco Company, but was completely neglected once the war had started. The internees could look across the Whangpoo River and see the buildings of the Bund, probably a painful sight that brought good memories of the past contrasting with their utter misery at present. However, some had made an effort to construct a garden among the junk and debris of preceding bombings which they christened "Happy Garden." There they managed to plant some vegetables and also clear a playing field. Later a number of women were transferred to Pootung from other camps. The total number of detainees reached 1,519. We also met another former Dodwell colleague of my father's. He too was gaunt, pale and unkempt. He mentioned that some internees participated in sports and a few musicians had organized a jazz band. His only happiness was listening to jazz, which he loved. Alas, one never knew when Japanese guards would suddenly cancel a performance.

In the once Restricted Area, the refugees were celebrating their survival in spite of the Nazis and the Japanese occupying forces. Now, the gates of their ghetto were thrown open, they could leave and return as they wished, no soldiers armed with bayonets were there to stop them. Dances, parties, celebrations were spontaneously organized.

But later, as news about the Holocaust and its millions of victims reached Shanghai, the atmosphere changed. Jewish refugees made desperate attempts to discover the fate of those they had left behind in Europe. The Red Cross was overwhelmed with people begging for information. Entire families had been gassed; surviving victims were in urgent need of serious rehabilitation and longed for a new home far from tyranny, far from unbearable memories. Could they leave Europe? Who would extend visas to them? Gloom and despair hit Shanghai Jews.

Today, Pootung (Pudong) is a very modern city with skyscrapers, broad roads, and elegant stores. Bridges as well as a tunnel connect it with the Bund. Comfortable ferries run regularly. At 7 o'clock in the evening, the Bund, as well as Pootung is lit up with beautiful neon lights, something nobody could imagine as a future possibility under Japanese occupation.

Chapter 24

U.S. FORCES ARRIVE

S hanghai was completely transformed. With the wave of a secret magic wand, the Japanese military became invisible. Suddenly hundreds of U.S. forces arrived. Most of them were from the China Burma India Theater (CBI). To us, the Air Force, Army and Navy men looked like Greek Gods descended from Mt. Olympus. They were tall, dressed in impeccable uniforms, full of high spirits and amazingly generous. Many were very young, most had been drafted and were not regular soldiers or sailors. They came from homes throughout the United States: in large cities, small towns, the countryside. After all they had endured, Shanghai, in spite of its wartime deterioration, appeared to them a modern metropolis full of wonders and beautiful women.

Traffic in Shanghai changed abruptly. No more *gazogenes*. Instead of Japanese camouflaged vehicles charging arrogantly through our city, dispersing local vehicles and pedestrians, happy smiling U.S. youngsters were driving a strange vehicle they called the "jeep." At first, we were not quite sure of the name, some pointed to them asking in a puzzled tone of voice: "Are these ugly things, the *peeps*, modern American cars?" Other vehicles rolling through our streets were weapons carriers and huge trucks called 6 x 6's. These gigantic trucks, which the GI's nicknamed *Deuce and a half*, were covered in the back with tarpaulin. Apparently, they could be used on the most rugged terrain.

No more Japanese troops, no more barricades and mysterious visitors in black cars surrounded by grim looking security motorcyclists, no more threats

Two happy GIs, 1946.

with bayonets, angry grunting and slaps on the face. People began to quickly fill in dug-outs and clean shop windows, attempting to restore order to our city. The entire population appeared to be stunned with surprise, relief and joy.

To participate in the excitement, my sister and I decided to go for a stroll. Very soon, two young Americans in uniform started following us. One said:

"Hi, Girls! Can we walk along with you?"

My sister, who was accustomed to more formal introductions and better manners, responded:

"What cheek!"

The Americans apparently didn't understand this English expression, so I clarified:

"She means you are very rude and impudent!"

They laughed, and the taller one replied:

"Sorry! We have been at the front for such a long time and we don't know any more how to behave any more with girls! I guess you thought we are 'fresh'. Please let us walk you home, if that's where you're going."

Flustered and curious, we agreed, then I asked:

"Are you aviators?"

They burst into laugher.

"We are just regular Air Force GI's, not brass."

We had never heard the word GI (initials for Government Issue), nor did we know what *brass* meant. We were to learn eventually many new expressions: *brass* for officers because of the small metal bars the lieutenants and captains wore on their shoulders, *chicken* for colonels because of the shape of their insignia, *swabee* for sailors who swabbed the decks, and an approving phrase for one's suggestion or action: "Now you're cooking on gas!"

When we got to our front door, my sister and I felt that we should ask them in out of courtesy. Our parents were very surprised by their arrival, greeted them warmly, offered them some Russian food, which it was quite obvious they found inedible. They asked if they could return the following day. They did, bringing cans of soup, meat, puddings, peaches and candy. We became friends and stayed friends until they returned to the United States.

We did not realize that they were very poorly educated. They knew nothing about China, nor Europe, but we on the other hand had never met Americans like them. They spoke with charming Southern accents because they came from Tennessee or Louisiana, were easy-going, good natured, uncomplicated boys who simply wanted to enjoy life.

A few days later, we took them along to a combination birthday/victory party at a very close friend's home. It was such a bubbly, happy affair. We danced, marched and played rather childish games, all the while laughing and acting silly. We sang at the top of our voices: "God Bless America!" and "We're Gonna Hang out the Washing on the Siegfried Line", as well as other songs forbidden during the Japanese occupation. Suddenly, after years of repression, all that young Shanghailanders wanted was fun, fun, fun.

Shortly after, members of General Claire Chennault's (1893–1958) "American Volunteer Group"(AVC), the *Flying Tigers*, began to appear in Shanghai. They belonged to transport and bomber units flying over the *Hump*, the nickname Americans had given to the Himalayas. Their mission: to stop Japanese aggression against China. My sister and I met several *Flying Tigers*. They were older than the very young GI's we knew, knowledgeable and educated. The *Flying Tigers* were personally trained by General Chennault who taught them tactics leading them to a record ten to one aerial kills against the Japanese. Thus, they succeeded in stopping the Japanese army's offensive along the Salween bank—a river running through deep gorges called by many *China's Grand Canyon*. It was the very first time that an invading army had ever been defeated by air power and made aviation history.

General Claire Chennault.

Between 20th Dec, 1941 and VJ (Victory over Japan) Day, General Chennault's AVC lost only 500 airplanes in combat while destroying 2,600 enemy planes. Some experts believe that probably 1,500 more planes could be added to this figure. The *Flying Tigers'* amazing achievement: sinking and damaging 2,230,000 tons of Japanese merchant shipping, 44 naval vessels and 13,000 river boats, destroying 500 bridges, and killing thousands of ground troops.

General Chennault was married to a very bright, attractive Chinese woman, Anna C. Chennault. She had the distinction of having been the first Chinese female reporter who, at the age of 20, was employed by the Central News Agency in China. After her marriage to General Claire Chennault, Mrs. Chennault became the first Chinese-American to work in the White House for six U.S. Presidents. In 1972 she was selected as one of America's 70 most influential people. By the time she died, she had written 53 books.

In 1946, I once rushed to the 4th floor window of Sassoon House where I had started working, propelled by very loud, raucous screaming from tremendous crowds massed on the Bund. A Japanese War Criminal was being driven to trial, standing on the back of on an open truck while thousands of people jeered. His hands were tied behind him, his face expressionless. I could see him very clearly as the truck moved slowly forward. Later, I learned that the prisoner was a Japanese officer who had participated in the trial and execution of U.S. airmen in accordance with Japan's "Enemy Airmen's Act," promulgated in April 1942 in response to the U.S. Doolittle raid on Japan. Now he, in turn, was being sentenced as a War Criminal by the Americans.

Chapter 25

JOBS, JOBS, JOBS

Shanghai began undergoing a complete transformation. Suddenly a great variety of jobs became available at, what appeared to be at the time, good salaries. The U.S. Forces and various U.N. organizations required clerical help, telex-typists, accountants, maintenance workers, mechanics, sales people for the Post Exchanges, cooks and servers for Enlisted Men's and Officers' Clubs, and entertainers for floor shows.

They also offered training courses since in Shanghai many skills, such as that of being a telex-typist, had been completely unknown. A whole new world was opening up to Shanghailanders and Shanghainese.

Once passing by a building occupied by the U.S. Army, my sister and I saw a big sign stating that telex courses would start in two weeks. People were invited to register for participation. On impulse, we went in and both signed up. I always wanted to learn something new and our normal lives—if one could call lives under Japanese occupation "normal" —were now completely disrupted. Like most of our friends, we felt we had been plunged into delightful unreality.

In addition to all the jobs available, some people even "invented" occupations for themselves. During the war, when I lay ill with typhoid in the Jewish Hospital, I was told an interesting story. There was a young Polish refugee who had arrived in Shanghai after many hair-raising escapes in Europe and had an accident that almost destroyed his legs. In Shanghai, he was hospitalized immediately. Some doctors recommended amputation that he fiercely rejected. He was prepared to use crutches all his life, but not to be

Picnic with friends. Author in dark sun-glasses.

legless. While being hospitalized, he noticed that many of the instruments used by nurses needed sharpening and reconditioning. Since he had a natural gift in his skillful hands for a variety of repairs, he volunteered to help. The result was impressive and, from that moment onwards, doctors and nurses kept him constantly busy. He lay in bed with a small table over his knees, glad to work productively.

When the war ended and the GIs arrived, opening a number of large Post Exchanges, the hospitalized man got an idea. The Post Exchanges sold a great number of watches and he decided to organize the creation of watch repair shops. He had never repaired a watch in his life—which, of course, he did not mention to those in charge of the PXs—but hired a number of Chinese watch repairmen whose detailed work he carefully checked and supervised. Of course, he had excellent recommendations from the hospital. In short, his success was remarkable and he became a rich man. Eventually, all armed forces were advised:

Watch Repair Available in all PX's

Other citizens of Shanghai, both foreign and Chinese, got jobs for which they were specifically trained and many advanced to very responsible positions. Preferential treatment was given to former "enemy nationals" who had been forced to wear armbands and had spent years in Japanese internment camps.

Hotels, nightclubs, restaurants and bars reopened all over the city. Most new employees were Chinese, European refugees, and stateless Russians. Foreign VIPs were usually lodged in the Cathay Hotel on the Bund. One should mention that, in medieval times, "Cathay" was the name given to China by English speakers. After the war, among prominent guests at the Cathay, were General George Catlett Marshall (1880–1959) and former U.S. President Herbert Hoover (1874–1964), who held meetings there.

In order to prevent friction between GIs and the local Chinese population, booklets were distributed individually to all U.S. forces, explaining how to behave and where to shop.

They stated that "the closest thing to Stateside food" was to be found at:

Jimmy's Kitchen—133 Nanking Rd.
Bakerit—833 Bubbling Well Rd. (Jing'ansi Lu today)

One must remember that most GIs had not received leave for over a year and had thus saved money, which they were now eager to spend. They were hungry to enjoy life and forget some of their terrible battle experiences. GIs now crowded restaurants and, as a result of their patronage, many restaurant and nightclub owners made small fortunes.

Regarding shopping, the advice as to how to deal with a salesman was:

A good rule to remember is, if you want it, establish the minimum price he will accept and then stop for a moment and coolly make up your mind whether the price represents what you are willing to pay. Make any difference to you? Once you decide you really want it, by all means buy it. It's Chinese, it's a memento of your stay in China, and it's a cinch that when you are back home, you will really prize it.

In recommendations as to where to buy, the booklet stated that there is no "infallible guide." First GIs were advised to look around at the Curio PX in Hamilton House on Kiangsi Road (Jiangxi Lu) and observe prices. After that, they should proceed to local stores of good repute.

Maximum speeds for vehicles in the Shanghai area were set at 15 miles per hour within the city limits, and 20 miles per hour outside of city limits. The only area "Out of Bounds" was the Chinese city, between the Rue des Deux Republiques (Renmin Lu today) in the North, the Whangpoo River in the South and East, and Minkuo Road (Renmin Lu today) in the West.

The GIs were billeted in big buildings, of which the Japanese had taken possession during their occupation of Shanghai after having evicted all residents.

Now individuals who had worked for Japanese propaganda were branded as traitors and got their due. Just as the war was about to end, Herbert Moy, a Chinese American who had broadcast for the German radio station XGRS died mysteriously. Others, depending on their nationality, were sent to Great Britain or America for trials. A Russian student I had known and who had collaborated with the Japanese disappeared and was not heard of again. All Japanese, civilians and military, were rounded up and sent to Japan. A few others were eventually arrested by the Soviets and sent to hard labor camps in the Soviet Union.

In my diary, on March 3, 1946, I wrote a poem reflecting my feeling of relief and contentment:

Clear night, bright stars in the sky,
A fire within the stove, the cats sitting like two balls,
The table set for five, the cook dressed in white,
Roast beef with peas, gravy and potatoes,
Spinach soup, salads and whipped cream dessert,
Steaming coffee, the radio playing dreamy tunes,
Mindless banter from young tongues,
Sleepy comfort, tired drowsiness.
The parents out to see a movie,
Sister's new beau smiling shyly,
My friend Jack at ease and content,
Grandmother sitting at table's head,
Speaking broken English,
With thick Russian accent,
Amah's tiny eyes above red cheeks,
Peering discretely at the boys.
Postwar night, youthful joys.

Chapter 26

DETERIORATION, DISTURBANCE

After the "happy honeymoon" with U.S. forces, rising problems marred the scene and resentment began to seep through the Shanghai population. The black market openly offered PX goods in stalls that mushroomed in streets all over our city. Popular brands of American cigarettes became available everywhere. Sometimes, crews of visiting U.S. Navy ships generously gave packs of Camel, Chesterfield and Lucky Strike to begging children, which their elders could easily convert into money. Thus, cigarettes were rapidly added to other black market merchandise. Today, old empty cans of Camel, Chesterfield and Lucky Strike dating back to the 1940's are offered for sale on the Internet. Collectors of memorabilia are eager to buy them. It was also a known fact that many GIs added to their income by selling cigarettes and other PX goods illegally. Besides, pilfering was common when U.S. Navy ships docked loaded with goods. Fortunes were made dishonestly, crooks became wealthy, but the lives of most hard-working laborers did not improve. My family, as far as I know, never bought anything on the Black Market. I must admit we were spoiled by the generosity of GI visitors who never failed to arrive bearing gifts of foods and other necessities legally purchased at various PXs. Both my parents were strictly against illegal acts of any kind, acts they considered dishonest and detrimental both to the Chinese and foreign population of Shanghai. Our cook continued going to the market and providing us with delicious meals consisting of locally grown vegetables, and local fowl, meat, and fish.

Since the Chinese currency kept depreciating, everyone, even rickshaw

A Chinese bank in Old Shanghai.

coolies and pedicab men, began demanding payment in U.S. dollars. By August 1948, U.S. $1.00 was valued at $12,000,000 in Chinese currency! This situation was intolerable and, as a result, the Central Bank of China introduced the "Gold Yuan." Under threat of arrest and even execution, citizens were forced to deliver all U.S. dollars and gold in their possession to the Central Bank. One Central Bank high official, who had not declared the strictly forbidden foreign currency and gold bars in his possession, was publicly executed on the Race Course. *Life* Magazine and other foreign media were permitted to photograph his execution.

The era of Extraterritorial Rights and Privileges had ended some years previously, in 1943. On January 11 of that year, the United States and Great Britain had signed an agreement with China, relinquishing all their special rights. The Declaration stated in part:

"The Treaty and accompanying exchange of notes, signed January 11, 1943, between the governments of the United States and China, provide for the relinquishment by the U.S. of extraterritoriality and other special privileges under which they had been hitherto exercising..."

After the war, it took months before the British Consulate moved back to their building on the Bund. The U.S. consular officials had to work for some time in rooms rented in the Park Hotel, until they finally returned to their original Development Building (corner of Kiangse and Foochow Rds.).

The French Concession was returned to China in mid 1943. Since my family lived in the French Concession, we became quickly aware of changes that were taking place. The French colony consisted of some 4,400 people: 2,400 civilians and 2,000 military and police. The French Concession was formally transformed into the 8th District of Shanghai. As the war was ending, the Japanese occupying forces became more and more aggressive and domineering. They requisitioned the *Cercle Français* (French Club) and the *College Municipal Français*, whose students were transferred to another French School—*Ecole Remi*. On July 19, 1945, Lt. Colonel Fabre, former Director of the French Concession police, shot himself in the head in his residence on Rue Stanislas Chevalier (Jianguo Zhonglu today). Some months later, his friend, Colonel Artigue who was very depressed by Fabre's self-imposed death, likewise attempted suicide by shooting himself in the head on the balcony of his office. He survived but because of resulting psychological problems and loss of memory, his life was destroyed. As almost all French privileges disappeared, the French colonists started leaving Shanghai.

Amazingly, Big Ears Du (Du Yue-Sheng) returned to his villa in the proximity of my family's home. Before the French Consul-General returned to France on holiday, Du invited him and other leading members of the French community to a farewell party. Following the festivities, it appeared that most of the foreign guests had been poisoned. As a result, several died as did the French Consul-General, who passed away in the ship on his way back to his homeland.

To us, old Shanghailanders, Shanghai was obviously in a stage of inescapable transition. My friends, my sister and I observed around us a general deterioration of morals. In the past, although we knew vice was rampant in Shanghai, we never really had paid attention to it. Now it was no longer possible to disregard its rapid development. The streets and entertainment spots were crowded with prostitutes (both Chinese and foreign), who openly pursued uniformed GIs. Many wore very tight dresses with deep decolletes, hardly ever seen before on the streets, walked seductively, beckoned publicly to men, sometimes rubbing their bodies close to them. We must have been naïve, but we had never noticed such open sexual behavior before. As to many GIs, they too fell into the trap, their behavior changed, they laughingly handed U.S. coins to Chinese beggar children who pursued them in groups, hands outstretched, shouting:

"No papa, no mama, no whiskey soda!"

Many responded willingly to the flaunting behavior of women.

As the civil war in China became more and more serious, wounded and hungry refugees kept fleeing into Shanghai and foreigners, uncertain the future, started preparing to abandon the city they had loved.

Chapter 27

UNITED NATIONS INFORMATION CENTER

O ne Sunday, I saw in the English paper an announcement that an essay competition was being held on the subject: *The Role of the Individual in the United Nations.* Since early youth, I had joined, whenever possible, literary and drawing competitions with successful outcomes. Excited by the challenge, I borrowed my mother's old typewriter and sat late at night at our dining room table, thinking, typing and retyping. Two weeks later the results came in: my essay had won an Honorary Mention, which opened the door for me to apply for a job at the United Nations Information Center, Shanghai. A new challenge! Now I was back in my world of learning and writing, ready to overcome new obstacles.

The man who interviewed me, the Information Officer, was a young, charming, bright, energetic Filipino named Jorge Teodoro. We immediately understood each other, had a lively conversation and Teodoro promised me a job as his secretary and general assistant. However, he warned me that the completion of formalities would take some time. Although it appeared an eternity to me, I was at my desk at the United Nations Information Center (UNIC) within a fortnight.

From the very beginning, my cooperation with Teodoro went smoothly. He was an excellent journalist who had worked for years as a newspaperman under General Romulo in Manila. Not only was our United Nations news gathering fascinating, but the number of top officials and journalists visiting us

The Bund, 1936.

kept me in a world of constant excitement, constant discovery and constant learning. Teodoro also took me along as translator to the USSR Consulate General and the French Consulate General.

"You know," he said, "Russians usually have a problem speaking English, and as to the French, they consider French as the world language of diplomats so they will be delighted that I brought you along."

The visits to the Russian and French Consulates General were always enlightening and extended my horizons. I would return home in the evening impatient to recount my experiences to my parents. The added excitement was that Teodoro owned a gorgeous yellow convertible, the only one of its kind at the time in Shanghai. When I sat at his side with curious crowds staring at our car—rather than at us—I felt like a fairy tale princess riding a golden chariot.

Teodoro also arranged for me to speak several times on radio programs, having as my partner a U.S. Airforce Officer with a very pleasant deep voice. Teodoro would always show me in advance the draft of a prepared text and ask me for my opinion. Totally inexperienced as I was, I felt remarkably comfortable on the radio, most probably because of the confidence Teodoro had in me, he always treated me respectfully as an equal.

Teodoro idolized General Carlos Romulo (1899–1985), a hero of World War II. Romulo was a Filipino diplomat, politician, soldier and—most important to Teodoro—journalist and author. He became a reporter at age 16, a newspaper editor at 20 and a publisher at 32! Moreover, he earned a number of degrees from well-known universities: doctorates in literature, in philosophy and law. Later, he served eight Filipino Presidents. From 1949–1950, he was elected President of the United Nations General Assembly.

Teodoro loved to tell the story how in 1948, at a U.N. Assembly held in Paris, when Andre Vishinsky, the USSR representative said deprecatingly to Romulo, who was 5'4 ft tall, as he presented his credentials:

"You are just a little man from a little country!"

To which Romulo replied with his usual eloquence:

"It is the duty of the little Davids of this world to fling the pebbles of truth in the eyes of blustering Goliaths and force them to behave!"

And when the U.N. seal representing the world was studied, U.S. Senator Warren Austin who headed the Committee stated:

Author having fun, 1940.

"Where is the Philippines? It's too small to include. If we put in the Philippines it would be no more than a dot."

Romulo firmly replied:

"I want that dot!"

After telling me these stories, Teodoro added:

"Look at the U.N. seal today. There is indeed a tiny dot between the Pacific Ocean and the South China Sea!"

There were a number of Chinese employees at the United Nations Information Center. We often had general meetings that were very productive. Most of the Chinese were young, enthusiastic, hard-working and some later reached high posts in various countries of the world.

In the midst of all the problems in Shanghai, we worked in an oasis of hope, friendship and joy.

On October 24, 1948, we celebrated United Nations Day.

This official celebration was to mark the coming into force of the UN Charter on October 24, 1945. The purpose of the celebration was to inform the world of the aims and achievements of the U.N. Organization.

Our celebration was a very jolly one. By then we all knew each other well, had developed friendships and enjoyed our work. For the occasion, I had my tailor Wu make me a lovely brocade dress.

In 1949, when my family had resettled in Israel, I received a very warm airmail letter from Jorge Teodoro. He wrote me he was leaving the following day with a group of observers for Korea where the danger of a deadly civil war was rapidly increasing. That was the last time I ever heard from him. His plane, filled with U.N. observers, was shot down over Korea. Nobody survived. Decades later, I saw his name memorialized at the Press Club in Tokyo.

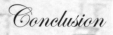

Conclusion

DEPARTURE AND RETURN

A s the civil strife in China increased and warfare rapidly approached
Shanghai, thousands of worried foreign inhabitants, as well as a
number of Chinese, felt trapped and sought for a way out to safety.
Now the main subjects of conversation became repatriation, immigration,
affidavits, visas and new beginnings.

The UNRRA (United Nations Relief and Rehabilitation Association) and
the IRO (International Refugee Organization) worked feverishly to help
those who wished to depart. U.S., British and French citizens were gradually
repatriated to their countries of origin.

For the Stateless, and others who hoped to rebuild new lives, visas to the
U.S., Australia, New Zealand or South and Middle America were extremely
difficult to obtain. The only country that responded positively to the plight
of some 5,500 White Russians (including a handful of Estonians) was the
Philippines. The island of Tubabao offered them a temporary refuge until
they were granted visas for other destinations. Some remained waiting for
three years.

In my family, my parents had considered immigrating to the United States,
but visa requirements were very complicated. Since quotas were based on the
applicant's place of birth, both my parents came under the Russian quota, but
my sister and I fell under the Chinese quota which was very restricted. As far
as my father was concerned, his deep desire had always been to live in Israel.
On May 14, 1948, Israel's Independence was officially declared and that same
evening the United States gave *de facto* recognition to the new State, followed

Last New Year Party in Shanghai on Dec.31, 1948. Author standing on the left, with her cousin and friends.

by *de jure* recognition by the U.S.S.R. All Jews immigrating to Israel would automatically receive, if they so desired, an Israeli passport.

Ultimately, Israel and the United States became the two countries which absorbed most Jews from China. Jewish refugees from Europe who had escaped Hitler were greatly assisted by American Jewish organizations such as the JDC (the Joint Distribution Committee) and HIAS (Hebrew Immigrant Aid Society).

Life in Shanghai had become very confusing. The rush to be repatriated, or to obtain visas throughout the world turned to panic. Foreigners preparing for departure had to sell at ridiculously low prices the possessions they could not take along: real estate, furniture, collections of paintings, Chinese porcelain and antique bronzes.

Early in April 1949, my family left for Israel. As we boarded our 4-engine Transocean Charter plane, the pilot asked if anyone would like to volunteer to be an assistant stewardess, I immediately raised my hand. I never could resist the opportunity of a new experience! I shall never forget our landing in Aden (Arabia) in the desert. Sand and camels greeted us. A plane was parked nearby waiting for another group of Jews from Yemen—*Operation Magic Carpet*—to board. The Yemenite Jews rushed towards us handing us oranges, welcoming us warmly in a language none of us understood, dragging us to dance with them in the sand. But soon it was time for them to leave. Climbing up the steps to the plane, they kept turning back, smiling and waving frantically to us.

We continued our journey with lighter hearts. The feeling of being forgotten and forsaken somewhere in the skies vanished. We knew we would be welcome in Israel.

45 years later, I was invited by Professor Pan Guang of the Center of Jewish Studies, Shanghai, and the Foreign Affairs Office, Shanghai Municipal People's Government, to participate in a seminar on April 21, 1994. Their wish: for me to make a presentation on Russian Jews in Shanghai.

It is hard to express the joy that overwhelmed me. Back home to Shanghai? At the same time my heart was gripped with apprehension. My parents had passed away, all my friends were gone and Shanghai must have become a totally different city. As we were about to land, I trembled with excitement but the moment my feet touched the earth, I knew I was at home.

Since then I have visited Shanghai a number of times, happy to observe the continuing improvement of life there, to see healthy children, well-dressed people on the streets, stores filled with a variety of goods, and to experience the general atmosphere of progress and optimism.

I am determined to return to the city of my youth again and again, rejoicing in the achievements of the Chinese people.

ACKNOWLEDGEMENT

I cannot end this book without extending my profound thanks to some of the numerous supporters who have so generously encouraged me. Among them are:

Michael Li, PhD (Shanghai) for his loyalty, support and affection, Prof. Christian Henriot (Lumiere-Lyon 2 University France, Stanford University and U.C. Berkeley) for his help, Consul General Gutman and his wife Avigail of the Israeli Consulate General in Shanghai for their support and cooperation, Archivist and Librarian Ron Bulatoff (Hoover Institution, Stanford) for his excellent assistance, Mohammad Alkhattat, my brilliant neighbor who solved the problems of my temperamental computer, Tess Johnston (Shanghai) for her interest and useful comments, enthusiastic friends Edith Benay, Karen Aparton, Carol and Ralph Pursifull, Rose Meller (California) and my dedicated husband, daughters and grand-children.

Rena Krasno